Leaders of the American Revolution

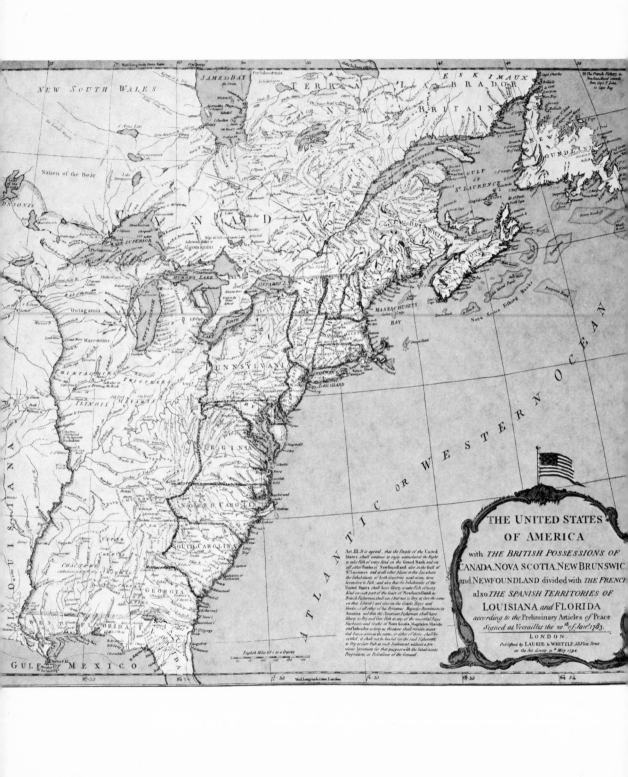

THE UNITED STATES
OF AMERICA
with *THE BRITISH POSSESSIONS OF*
CANADA, NOVA SCOTIA, NEW BRUNSWIC
and NEWFOUNDLAND divided with *THE FRENCH*
also *THE SPANISH TERRITORIES OF*
LOUISIANA and FLORIDA
according to the Preliminary Articles of Peace
Signed at Versailles the 20ᵗʰ *of* Janʳ *1783.*

LONDON
Published by LAURIE & WHITTLE, 53 Fleet Street
as the Act directs 12ᵗʰ May 1794.

Leaders
of the
American Revolution

by LeRoy Hayman

FOUR WINDS PRESS/NEW YORK

Second Printing 1972
First Printing 1970

Published by Four Winds Press
A Division of Scholastic Magazines, Inc., New York, N.Y.
Copyright © 1970 Scholastic Magazines, Inc.
All Rights Reserved
Printed in the United States of America

Library of Congress Catalogue Card Number: 79-124186

For Dr. Joseph Tarkington,
whose hand guides mine

Contents

In the late 1600's it was the "City of New York in the Province of New York, North America." Once owned by the Dutch, it was now the property of the English—who boasted that the "Trade of the City in a few years is become almost universal, her Merchants having extended their Commerce to most parts of ye known World." LIBRARY OF CONGRESS

The War Before the War

It was a fair land, even fairer than their native England. After weeks at sea crossing the stormy North Atlantic, the Pilgrims came ashore from the *Mayflower* to a bleak and icebound New England coast. They soon sensed, however, that the oncoming spring would turn this winter landscape into a green and flowering countryside. And they knew at once, despite the forbidding cold, that this was to be home. They were here to stay.

So too it was with many of the English colonists who had landed in Virginia some years earlier. To be sure, there were gentlemen fortune-hunters among them, men who had come only to gather the gold that was said to be lying all about. Then they intended to return to England with their wealth, buying their way into society. But there were also

[9]

poor men—including released convicts and people who had "indentured" themselves (agreed to act as servants for many years in order to earn their fare)—who had come to build a new life in a new land. The fortune-hunters never found their gold, but the poor men won a place for themselves in the New World.

Slowly, slowly, slowly these Englishmen—and others who followed: the Scotch-Irish, the Dutch, the Germans, the French Huguenots, the Swedes—became Americans. Long before the American Revolution gave the colonists their own nation and their own nationality, many of them had become Americans in fact. They took on the color of the country, and in time it became their own, to be passed down to their children and their children's children.

This American coloration was the result of an accumulation of encounters the colonists had with their British masters, with the New World French, with the Indians, and with the land itself. Each event added something to the colonists' stature, to their sense of independence, to their sense of control over their environment and destiny.

One such event took place a hundred years before the American Revolution started. It was an earlier war, this one confined to New England. The struggle was no turning point, no prelude to revolt, by itself. It was instead only one of the many incidents which gradually led to the colonial overthrow of an increasingly oppressive regime.

The war was fought between the Puritan colonists and the Indians. It was called King Philip's War, named for one of the Algonquin chiefs who led the marauding tribesmen.

The conflict had its roots in the fact that the Puritan and the Algonquin ways of life were very different. For a long time, white and red men had lived side by side in southern New England—but without actually becoming friends and neighbors. Many Indians, however, had become Christians— they were called "Praying Indians"—and most of them, Christian or not, did business with their Puritan neighbors. They sold fish, game, canoes, and wicker baskets to the settlers— and sometimes they "sold" their lands as well.

But the Indian's idea of selling land was not like the white man's. Legally, the Indians held title to their land in common, and no single tribesman owned a particular plot of ground. The Indians' notion of a land transaction was no more than a kind of rental or leasing arrangement, for which they were paid so many pots, hatchets, or blankets. What was more, the Indians meant to go on living on the land during the time the colonists were paying rent for it—and to collect more utensils and tools when the original ones were lost or broken.

The Puritans, however, insisted that a sale was a sale and began crowding the Indians off the property. One Algonquin tribe, the Wampanoags, grew incensed at this treatment. Their chief, Metacom, whom the colonists called King Philip, had sold the settlers much land with the idea that his people would continue living on it.

Not so, said the Puritans, and proceeded to take over their purchases. King Philip showed his resentment of all this, and was thereupon accused of plotting against Plymouth Colony. For these alleged offenses he was three times brought into court and fined.

The plot accusation was actually the work of King Philip's own Indian aide, Sassamon, who had informed on his leader. For this treachery Sassamon was assassinated by his fellow tribesmen. But the Puritans acted swiftly. The assassins were

[11]

duly caught, tried, and executed. Their deaths brought on King Philip's War.

On June 24, 1675, the Wampanoags raided the Puritan settlement at Swansea, on Mount Hope, Narragansett Bay. King Philip and his warriors escaped after their raid by fleeing into Massachusetts. With the Nipmuck tribe, they proceeded to attack the frontier settlements of Brookfield, Lancaster, Deerfield, and others. The news of Indians on the warpath spread swiftly, and the whole New England Confederacy, including the Connecticut Colony, was up in arms against the Algonquins.

The Indians continued their savage raids on the isolated westernmost settlements, and it seemed for a time as if King Philip's braves would kill every white settler in New England. The Algonquins swooped down on the English communities time after time. They burned and looted the houses and barns, slaughtered all the livestock they did not intend to carry away, and fired at every colonist who ventured into the open.

The Algonquins were experts with the musket. They killed many settlers, including women and children. But the white people could not stay cooped up in their garrison buildings forever. They had to tend crops and care for their livestock. When they did so, they risked being picked off by Indian marksmen.

The Indians, however, were hit-and-run warriors. They did not stick at the business of fighting, nor did they follow through on their gains. It was enough for them to raid one settlement at a time, then retreat to enjoy their booty. Moreover, the various tribes in New England—Wampanoag, Pequot, Mohegan, Penacook, and others—did not join forces.

As seen by a colonial artist and engraver, rural America was sweet and self-sufficient. At left, a waterwheel powered a saw for turning logs into boards. Boats sailed along the river at center. And at right, a two-wheeled cart and a horseman approach the manor house through an open field. LIBRARY OF CONGRESS

Instead, each tribe stayed in its own area and had little to do with the others, and many of the Praying Indians actually fought alongside the colonists.

For their part, the colonies had alert governors. In the autumn of 1675, Governors Jon Leverett, John Winthrop, Jr., and Josiah Winslow decided to launch a massive counter-attack against the Narragansetts, who were believed to be sheltering a number of Wampanoags. (The descendants of these governors and others are still leaders in present-day New England.)

They appointed Governor Winslow to lead a company of about one thousand well-armed colonists across to Narragansett Bay, then inland to Rhode Island. The settlers pounced upon some three thousand Narragansetts and engaged them in furious fighting, and for three hours the battle raged back and forth.

Finally the Narragansetts gave up. Leaving about two thirds of their number dead on the battlefield, they retreated to a position of safety. Winslow's men fell back and counted their own dead—eighty slain, including eight senior officers. But the Narragansetts were decisively defeated, even though the war continued in other areas of New England.

(The remaining three hundred-odd Narragansetts took cover that winter in a fort hidden deep in the Rhode Island forest. The following spring they came forth to resume their traditional routine of fishing, lobstering, and clamming in Narragansett Bay. As they prepared to move toward the shore, they were attacked by a troop of Connecticut mounted militia who appeared on the scene. The horsemen mowed down 228 of the Indians and left those still alive without their chiefs.)

King Philip retreated to Mount Hope and was surrounded by a band of armed colonists and their Indian allies. When Philip tried to breach the circle, he was slain. Thus King Philip lost his war, and the power of the hostile Indians was broken for a long time.

The colonists' victory, however, was a costly one. It took twenty years to rebuild the ravaged villages, and there was no westward movement by the settlers for another forty years.

Why then was King Philip's War and the colonial victory important? For one thing, it showed that the settlers no longer depended on English troops to protect and defend them. It demonstrated that they could get along on their own, that they were ready to fight for their families and their possessions.

In a sense, the war indicated that by the 1670's the colonists were already preparing for independence. It showed that strong colonial leaders were coming forth, men whose descendants would direct the confrontations and the conflicts in the grim years between 1775 and 1783.

Valiant James Otis strikes an impressive pose. NEW YORK PUBLIC LIBRARY

1761—"American independence was then and there born…"

When did the American Revolution begin? It started much earlier than 1775, when the actual fighting broke out. As early as King Philip's War a century before, the colonists were already staking out their claims to independence. But few, if any, realized that they were doing so.

In this New World the colonists were building a new society. Yet for long decades they continued to regard themselves as loyal British subjects, devoted to their king, obedient to Parliament's laws. Their home was in America, but their hearts were in England.

There was no single point at which the colonists began to lose their British loyalty and look upon themselves as Americans. The shift was gradual; and for some, the thousands of Loyalists who fled to Canada during and after the fighting, the transfer was never made at all.

Yet one event stands out in those hectic years before the Revolution. It was the occasion when James Otis, a Massachusetts lawyer, defiantly attacked the British Parliament for its attempt to impose *writs of assistance* on the colonists. The writs were to give British authorities unrestricted license to search and seize the colonists' possessions. The year was 1761.

At the time Otis, just turned thirty-six, was a prosperous and, until then, a peaceful citizen. He was a man whose people had been in Massachusetts for 130 years. John Otis, his grandfather, had settled in Barnstable, Massachusetts, and had served as judge and as commander of the county militia. John Otis's son, James, also held military rank and was a lawyer, besides. James' son, also named James, was the oldest of thirteen children.

The boy was born in his grandfather's big house at the Great Marshes, West Barnstable. It was on Cape Cod, where the wind carried the salt smell of the sea right through the open windows. Young James learned to read at a dame school, a class conducted for young children by a woman of the neighborhood who knew little more than how to read and do simple arithmetic herself. James was glad to flee from her gentle tyranny into the woods and marshes surrounding his grandfather's house. In time, however, he settled down to his studies, knowing that he was expected to carry on the family tradition and practice law.

James studied under the local minister, then entered Harvard College in his early teens. The courses were hard and the college rules restrictive. But James managed to have a bit of fun—climbing in through a window after the residence hall was locked up for the night, throwing snowballs at his professors, even smuggling in a noggin of rum, a drink forbidden the students.

Most of his courses were Greek or Latin, which were suitable for those who were preparing for the ministry or the law. (Few others in the colonies went to college or even studied under their ministers.) James was graduated from Harvard in 1743 at the age of eighteen.

To become a lawyer himself, a young man "read" law in an established lawyer's office. This meant that the lawyer-to-be studied the meager texts on the lawyer's bookshelves, learned how to prepare legal papers, followed his mentor to court and watched him argue a case—in short, absorbed theory and practice in somewhat the same way as an apprentice learned the silversmith's trade and art.

JAMES OTIS

Like silversmithing, the practice of law was both trade and art. It involved such everyday chores as transferring ownership of property from seller to buyer. It also involved the fine art of arguing for a legal decision that might someday be the law of the land.

Young Otis enthusiastically began studying law under a noted colonial attorney named Jeremiah Gridley. He was admitted to the bar of Plymouth County at the age of twenty-three, and in 1750 he settled in Boston to practice. Five years later he married Ruth Cunningham, daughter of a wealthy Boston merchant. They had a son and two daughters.

At first Otis was no defiant radical. He had a prosperous practice, especially in civil and in admiralty law, dealing with ships and shipping. (For this his foes later called him a "smugglers' lawyer.") At the same time he indulged in a learned hobby, the study of Latin and Greek poetry. He

[19]

also read widely in English literature and in studies of political theory. Things were going well with him—the royal governor appointed him the king's advocate general of the Vice-Admiralty court in Boston. This meant that he represented the government's interests in court cases that dealt with shipping.

In 1756 Britain was drawn into a war with France, fought largely on the American frontier but with some battles overseas as well—in far-off India, for example. This French and Indian War, as it was called in America, was a struggle for possession of the North American continent. It had French and French-Canadian soldiers and their Indian allies on one side, and British regular troops and colonial militia on the other. The struggle seesawed for years, and the drain on the British treasury was heavy. William Pitt, the British prime minister, and Parliament looked for ways to get money from the colonies to help finance the war.

In 1760 Pitt thought he found a way. He ordered that the Sugar Act be enforced to the letter. Passed back in 1733, the Sugar Act put a heavy duty, or tax, on molasses imported into the colonies from the French and Spanish West Indies. The molasses was used to make New England rum, and the rum was traded for African slaves.

This three-way, or triangular (New England-Africa-West Indies), trade was the backbone of New England's prosperity. Much of the prosperity was derived from the fact that the Sugar Act tax had been successfully evaded ever since its passage. Now its enforcement was threatening to cost many Boston merchants much money.

The unpopular law, however, proved hard to enforce. To help apply the provisions of the Sugar Act, the king's customs officers in Boston asked the Superior Court of Massachusetts for writs of assistance. These writs were like search warrants, permitting a customs officer to inspect a house, barn, shed, warehouse—any place in fact where the illicit molasses might be hidden.

Now many New Englanders realized that smuggling molasses was against the law, and they were not especially happy about breaking it. But evading customs duties was one thing —and using writs of assistance to invade private property on the mere suspicion of evasion was quite another. The first was considered only a minor sin. The second was judged an outright violation of the fundamental rights of a free-born British subject, a violation that was being sanctioned because he happened to live in the colonies. The colonists were outraged.

JAMES OTIS

No one was angrier than James Otis. He quit his post as King's advocate general early in 1761 to protest the issuing of the writs in a dramatic courtroom appearance. Young John Adams, who was to play such an important part in American history himself, heard Otis speak before the Superior Court. Adams, in his old age recalling Otis's magnificent performance, said: "American independence was then and there born; the seeds of patriots and heroes were then and there sown."

Otis opened his argument by thundering, ". . . I will to my dying day oppose with all the powers and faculties God has given me all such instruments of . . . villainy . . . as this writ of assistance is." He went on to condemn the writ as "universal"—that it was aimed at every Englishman, whether or not there were grounds for suspecting a crime. A writ in the hands of an officer turned him into a tyrant who could "control, imprison, or murder anyone . . ." and be "account-able to no person for his doings."

Using all his lawyer's eloquence, Otis went on: "Now, one of the most essential branches of English liberty is the free-dom of one's house. A man's house is his castle; and while he is quiet, he is as well guarded as a prince in his castle. This writ, if it should be declared legal, would totally annihi-late this privilege." Otis was arguing for the common law, the basic system of justice upon which the British legal and social structure was built. Not the king nor the prime min-ister, not the Parliament nor all the judges in the land, could take away these basic rights from Englishmen. The common law for Britain was and is like the Constitution of the United States.

Otis lost his case—temporarily. Reviewing the case five years later, however, the British attorney general, De Gray, ruled that the enforcement of the Sugar Act did not author-ize the use of writs of assistance in the colonies. As the tide of Revolution grew stronger, colonial leaders invoked Otis's arguments that colonies could not be treated as second-class citizens in England's "green and pleasant land." They were entitled to the same rights and privileges as every other Englishman. Otherwise, they said. . .

Long before the attorney general's favorable decision, how-ever, Otis got himself embroiled in a new controversy. It was 1764, and the French and Indian War had been settled for more than a year. The war had won for Britain virtually all of Canada, all of the Louisiana Territory that lay east of the Mississippi (with the exception of New Orleans), plus certain French holdings in India. Britain was rich in new lands, but the victory had taken all its ready cash. The royal treasury was bare.

In its early days Harvard "Colledge" had three buildings—Harvard Hall, Stoughton Hall, and Massachusetts Hall—where students were housed, fed, and instructed, and from which they sometimes played hookey.

James Otis receives the acclaim of his fellow Bostonians after taking his stand before the Superior Court.

Young King George III, only twenty-six, had been on the throne for four years. He was determined to rule. He was equally determined not to be the puppet of Parliament and his ministers, as George II, his grandfather, had been. Inspired by the victory in the French and Indian War, he had a new vision of empire. The vision did *not* include the thirteen American colonies as equal partners in the empire. The colonies were considered to be only possessions, ranking with lands taken as spoils of war.

The king's new prime minister, George Grenville, was determined to collect long-overdue taxes from the colonies. The war, Grenville reasoned, had been fought largely to protect the American colonies. Why shouldn't they help pay for it?

The colonies had been hit by taxes before. But even the old Sugar Act had been meant mainly as a way of controlling trade. Grenville's new Revenue Act was Parliament's first try at taxing the colonies directly for the purpose of raising money. The law said so in so many words: ". . . a revenue raised in Your Majesty's dominions in America for defraying the expenses of defending, protecting, and securing the same."

The Atlantic seaboard again buzzed with angry demonstrations. Taxes to regulate and control business were one thing, and taxes for revenue, money-raising, were quite another. This second kind of tax, the colonists argued, must not be passed without the colonies' consent. Yet how could they give their consent if there were no colonial representatives in Parliament? Here was the nub of the argument: can a legislature impose taxes—or any other kind of law—upon the people, if the people's delegates are not members of that legislature? It was a cry raised over and over again until the Revolution itself began: "Taxation without representation is tyranny!"

Otis sat down and wrote a blistering pamphlet called *The Rights of the British Colonies Asserted and Proved.* In it he hammered home one point over and over again. The point was simply this: "Every British subject born on the continent of America or in any other of the British dominions is by the law of God and nature, by the common law, and by *JAMES OTIS* act of Parliament . . . entitled to all the natural, essential, inherent, and inseparable rights of our fellow subjects in Great Britain." And, he went on to say, "no man or body of men, not excepting the Parliament, justly, equitably and consistently with their own rights and the constitution can take [them] away."

Otis's fiery words helped sow the seeds of revolution. If the colonies could not send representatives to Parliament, he was suggesting, then the colonies would be better off on their own. Only a decade later, the colonies put Otis's suggestion into practice.

This was Otis's finest hour. He later took a moderate part in the agitation against the Stamp Act and the Townshend Act. In the 1770's, however, he began acting in ways that showed that he might be insane. His death was as dramatic as his denunciations of Parliament had been—in 1783 he was struck down by a bolt of lightning.

Fiery Patrick Henry, who was not often observed in such repose. NEW YORK PUBLIC LIBRARY

1765—"Caesar had his Brutus..!"

Whenever they could, the American colonists avoided or evaded Grenville's Revenue Act. The British Parliament, seeing that the act was producing little cash, determined to levy a stronger tax. On March 22, 1765, it passed the Stamp Act "for . . . applying certain stamp duties . . . in the British colonies and plantations in America, toward further defraying the expenses of defending, protecting, and securing the same. . ."

This new Stamp Act was ready to impose heavy taxes, involving the purchase of stamps that had to be pasted on all sorts of printed matter — every kind of legal document, diploma, warrant, deed, license, even playing cards and dice, before they could be sold. Every copy of every newspaper and almanac required a stamp, and the stamps were by no means cheap. The diploma stamp was to cost two pounds, the liquor sales license stamp twenty shillings.

The Stamp Act was to go into effect on November 1, 1765. By this time, however, the colonies were so well united in protest against the hated tax that it was never put into action. Men in every seaport town up and down the coast organized themselves into groups called the "Sons of Liberty." They raided the stamp offices, burned the stamps, talked (or frightened) the stamp officers into quitting, and never let the stamp tax collection get started.

In New York City, for example, on that November 1, the Sons of Liberty chased the British lieutenant-governor into hiding aboard a British warship anchored in the harbor. Then they swarmed into the governor's coach house, wrecked his carriages, and burned the stamps waiting to be sold.

One of the British officers had announced earlier that he was going to "cram the Stamp Act down the people's throats." The Sons of Liberty marched to his house and virtually pulled it down, and destroyed its contents. They trampled down his garden, drank his wine and whiskey, and left carrying his regimental flag before them as a final defiant touch.

The rioting and rebellion against the Stamp Act was repeated everywhere. The colonies had never before been so united in their protest and demonstration. What brought them together this time?

At first some of the colonial leaders were inclined to obey the Stamp Act. The Massachusetts legislature voted to go along with it. Ben Franklin said it had to be obeyed. But a young member of the Virginia House of Burgesses (the lower house of the Virginia colonial legislature) thundered

The Latin phrase on the infamous Stamp Act stamp is ironically translated: "Shame be to him who thinks evil."

NEW YORK PUBLIC LIBRARY

It was before the Virginia House of Burgesses that Patrick Henry voiced his "Caesar had his Brutus ..!" challenge.

NEW YORK PUBLIC LIBRARY

his opposition to it. His voice was heard throughout the colonies—and helped unite them to fight the tax.

That young man was twenty-nine-year-old Patrick Henry, serving his first term in the Virginia lawmaking body. He had been a member for only nine days when on May 30, 1765, he decided to speak out against the despised tax that was to take effect the following November. He offered twelve resolutions, the fifth of which brought forth his immortal plea for resistance. Arguing for this resolution, Henry asserted the *colonial* legislatures had the "sole and exclusive right" of taxation, and every move to deny this was a move that would rob not only Americans of their freedom, but Britons as well.

The debate over this fifth resolution grew hot. Henry got to his feet and began defending it, attacking its attackers. Soon he came to his fighting climax: "Tarquin and Caesar each had his Brutus, Charles the First his Cromwell, and George the Third . . ." Henry paused to let his words sink in.

Before he could start again, there came the cry, "Treason! Treason!" His audience picked up the cry and repeated it again and again. Henry was ready for the accusation.

Picking up where he left off, he said coolly, ". . . may profit by their example. *If this be treason, make the most of it!*"

Henry's bold challenge won the House to his point of view. The resolution passed—and more important, his words, carried by messengers across the thirteen colonies, inspired them to act as one against the tax. Did the American Revolution start here? It may very well have.

Patrick Henry went on to positions of leadership and influence in the colonies and, after the Revolution, in the new United States. Yet he began as an ambling country boy whose early years showed no promise of his later performance.

John Henry, Patrick's father, was a Scotsman who had come from Aberdeen after being graduated from King's College in that city. He settled on a farm north of Richmond near a little community called Haw's Shop. Patrick, born in 1736, was one of two sons and seven daughters. The boy went to common school until he was ten. Thereafter his only teachers were his father and his uncle, an Anglican minister.

The boy was a born talker but showed little ability at anything else. When he was fifteen his father put him to work in a country store. Patrick proved himself a poor storekeeper. Despite this, he and his brother soon started a store of their own. This enterprise closed its doors after a little time. Too often the brothers were talking when they should have been serving customers.

Young Henry was only eighteen when he married Sarah Shelton, only sixteen. As a wedding present Sarah's father gave the teenage couple a three-hundred-acre farm, complete with a house and six black slaves. Like the store, the farm eventually went under, as did, a little later, another store. By this time Henry was the father of four. How was he going to support them?

Henry determined to turn his ability to talk into a vocation. He decided to become a lawyer. After "reading" law in an attorney's office (as had James Otis) for only a little while, he applied at Williamsburg for admission to the bar. The examiners were skeptical of his scanty prepatation, but in the end gave Henry his license to practice —after he promised faithfully to keep on studying.

With his lawyer's license in hand, Henry was a new

man. He practiced his profession energetically in his little Virginia crossroads town called Hanover Court House and soon was earning respectable fees. In 1763 he scored a small but interesting victory in the courts for the cause of freedom in the colonies.

The case was called "The Parsons' Cause," because it involved the clergymen of Virginia. These men had long collected their pay in so many pounds of tobacco, which in a bad crop year skyrocketed in price. Even in a good crop year the tobacco never fell below a reasonable price. The men of the cloth liked this arrangement and were put out when the House of Burgesses passed a law saying that payment could be made either in money or tobacco, whichever was the cheaper.

Feeling that they were being cheated out of what was rightfully theirs, the parsons sent a hot protest to London. Soon they received the good news that George III had vetoed the law. For their audacity in passing it, the House of Burgesses and the Virginia governor received a vigorous tongue-lashing from the king.

The clergymen promptly filed suit in several Virginia counties for their back pay. One of the suits took place at Hanover Court House, with Patrick Henry as attorney for the counties. Speaking first, the parsons' lawyer advised the jury that there was no argument and that the jury's only job was to decide how much the clergymen were going to be paid.

Then Henry got up. He never made a good first impression—he was thin, shabby, and a poor speaker before he warmed up—yet he soon captured the attention of his listeners. He did not plead the injustice of the parsons'

Philadelphia's Independence Hall, on the eve of the American Revolution, was the headquarters of the First Continental Congress. It was soon to house the wartime Second Continental Congress and, a decade later, the Constitutional Convention that would write the nation's charter. FREE LIBRARY OF PHILADELPHIA

Here, before the Virginia Convention, Patrick Henry uttered his magnificent "Give me liberty or give me death!" NEW YORK PUBLIC LIBRARY

cause. Instead he attacked the king, who, from his palace across the sea, had vetoed a law that the colony had passed. He argued that a king who would do this was no longer a father to his people but a tyrant who was not to be obeyed. The parsons and their lawyers tried to fight back, but the jury took his argument as gospel truth. It soon brought in a verdict of one penny in damages awarded to the ministers.

Henry had struck his first blow for liberty. His fellow Virginian, Tom Jefferson, later said, "Mr. Henry certainly gave the first impulse to the ball of revolution."

A year and a half later came Henry's immortal "If this be treason . . ." speech to the Virginia House of Burgesses —sending the ball of revolution rolling even more swiftly. He continued battling the oppressive measures imposed by the king and Parliment. Although he was not yet ready to see the colonies take up arms against them, he fought the British authorities harder and harder in the courts and legislature.

Virginia's Committee of Correspondence, which had its counterparts in several other colonies, became especially active in the early 1770's. The committee was the colonies' first attempt to work together outside British control and supervision. In 1774 it was instrumental in organizing a group of delegates from all colonies to meet in an annual congress. Henry and several others, including George Washington, were chosen to attend the first meeting as Virginia delegates.

The First Continental Congress met September 5, 1774, in Philadelphia, in the little building later to be known as Independence Hall. On the second day Henry rose to speak on a vital question: whether the voting should be by colonies or by individuals. He made his point in a dramatic speech ending: "All America is thrown into one mass . . . The distinctions between Virginians, Pennsylvanians, New Yorkers, and New Englanders are no more. I am not a Virginian, but an American!"

As he had done before, Patrick Henry had defined the issue, provided the firm base from which useful discussion could proceed. John Adams later wrote of this meeting: "There was not one member except Patrick Henry who appeared to me sensible of the precipice, or rather, the pinnacle on which he stood, and had the candour and the courage to admit it."

The Congress lasted more than a month. Then the delegates left for home. Home for Henry was now a handsome 1,000-acre estate called Scotchtown, located near Hanover Court House. It was a place to which he would return again and again between summonses to action.

This time he had only five months to call his own. His next political meeting, in March 1775, was the Virginia Convention held in St. John's Church at Richmond. Richmond was chosen instead of the capital city of Williamsburg in order to avoid the influence of the royal governor, the many families loyal to Britain, and the British warships anchored in the harbor.

As far as Henry was concerned, the meeting gave too much consideration to the British side of the developing conflict. He soon demanded that Virginia set up a systematic plan of armed defense with an organized militia. Once again he had defined the issue—but this time he was hotly opposed. Other members were all for liberty, they claimed, but not many were ready as yet to fight for it.

[35]

Henry took the floor. As he warmed to his argument he demanded "to know what there has been in the conduct of the British ministry for the last ten years, to justify those hopes with which gentlemen have been pleased to solace themselves and the House?" He went on to demonstrate that Britain's "navies and armies" were in America to put down by force any move towards freedom. America had no recourse except to fight: "I repeat it, sir, we must fight! An appeal to the God of Hosts is all that is left of us!"

And he closed with an impassioned plea, one of the noblest and most inspiring cries for freedom ever voiced:

It is in vain, sir, to extenuate the matter. Gentlemen may cry peace, peace—but there is no peace. The war is actually begun! The next gale that sweeps from the north will bring to our ears the clash of resounding arms! Our brethren are already in the field. Why stand we here idle? What is it that gentlemen wish? What would they have? Is life so dear, or peace so sweet, as to be purchased at the price of chains and slavery? Forbid it, Almighty God! I know not what course others may take; but as for me, give me liberty or give me death!

Henry's rousing demands brought the convention around to his thinking. It voted to set up a colonial defense system and to recruit a militia. The action was taken none too soon, for the next month the fighting began with the clash of arms at Lexington and Concord in Massachusetts.

Although Henry never matched these fiery words again, his service to Virginia and his country went on. In May 1776 he was appointed chairman of a committee to write

of such laws, are generally dangerous, and ought to be avoided.

N. B. It is proposed to make some alteration in this last article when reported to the house. Perhaps somewhat like the following

That all laws having a retrospect to crimes, & punishing offences committed before the existence of such laws are dangerous, and ought to be avoided, except in cases of great & evident necessity, when the safety of the state absolutely requires them. — This is thought to state with more precision the doctrine respecting ex post facto laws & to signify to posterity that it is considered not so much as a law of right, as the great law of necessity, which by a well known maxim is allowed to supersede all human institutions.

Another is agreed to in committee condemning the use of general warrants; & one other to prevent the suspension of laws, or the execution of them.

The above clauses, with some small alterations, & the addition of one or two more, have already been agreed to in the committee appointed to prepare a declaration of rights, when this business is finished in the house, the committee will proceed to the ordinance of government. T. L. Lee —

This is a portion of the original draft of the Virginia Declaration of Rights, the document that foreshadowed the Bill of Rights—the first ten amendments to the U.S. Constitution. LIBRARY OF CONGRESS

a constitution for Virginia. The group produced a constitution that became a model for other state charters and eventually for the U.S. Constitution itself.

The Virginia constitution was especially notable for its bill of rights. Long before the first ten amendments—the federal Bill of Rights—were added to the U.S. Constitution in 1791, the Virginia bill spelled out the basic rights that every man is entitled to. Virginia's Declaration of Rights said:

—— that power is vested in and thus must come from the people;

—— that leaders must answer to the people;

—— that a state had a right to keep its militia;

—— that no soldier in peacetime could be quartered in a private house without the owner's consent;

—— that the people had the right to be secure and safe from unauthorized searches and seizures;

—— that the press must be free;

—— that all people had the right to say what they think.

When Virginia became a state in 1776, Henry was chosen governor. His wife, Sarah, had died, leaving his six children motherless. Henry married again, this time to Dorothea Dandridge, who was to bear him eleven more children. The family moved their home to an estate of several thousand acres in Henry County, named for him.

Henry was reelected governor in 1777 and 1778, but turned down a fourth consecutive term. For the next decade he alternated between the governor's mansion and the legislature. He served as a delegate to the Constitutional Convention in 1787 and fought hard for a bill of rights in the new U.S. Constitution.

[38]

The other delegates did not heed his plea and submitted the "right-less" Constitution to the states for ratification. Henry thereupon took his fight to the Virginia ratifying convention, demanding that the Constitution be turned down until such a bill was included. Virginia, however, went ahead with ratification.

But Henry's battle was not lost. The first work of the First Congress that assembled in 1789 was to pass the first ten amendments to the Constitution. When these ten were ratified by the states, the Bill of Rights was fixed as part of the national charter.

PATRICK HENRY

Henry remained active in politics for the rest of his life, largely as an elder statesman. He died in 1799, one of the great builders of the new nation.

*John Adams was as comfortable in his quiet library
as he was in a crowded courtroom.* NEW YORK PUBLIC LIBRARY

1770—"The law...will preserve a steady, undeviating course..."

Some patriots, such as James Otis, whooshed on and off the Revolutionary scene like meteors. Others served their country with a quieter devotion that spanned decades. One of these was John Adams.

Adams' first great public service took place in 1770. Thirty years later he finished his term as second President of the United States. Until his death in 1826 he was one of America's elder statesmen, making wise and pungent comments on the development of the nation he had served so long.

In 1770 Adams was thirty-five years old. He was a Boston lawyer who had become caught in the groundswell of revolt ever since the hated Stamp Act five years before had threatened colonial rights. Like many other colonists—but not all— he resented the growing governmental intrusions on his right to think and act as a free-born British subject.

Yet John Adams was also a man who believed in law and justice. It was for the sake of law and justice that he turned his back on his patriot friends and defended the cause of nine British soldiers involved in what history has misnamed the "Boston Massacre."

Every age and every society has its protest groups—only the names, not the characters, change. Most of these protest groups have legitimate grievances, protested against in acceptable ways. But many of these groups also have "far-out" elements, interested only in the ruckus and rioting they can cause. Boston in 1770 was no exception.

In order to exist, "far-outers" need someone to pick on, preferably someone who is close at hand and highly visible. In this case the "far-outers" were a young and roving band of Boston colonists, the radical fringe of the more disciplined and purposeful Sons of Liberty. The victims were the British troops posted around town as guards and sentries.

The "far-outers" did have something of a point—the presence of the troops was a sign that the British king and the Parliament regarded the Bostonians as rebels and insurgents. But the soldiers were only following their routine. They were apparently singled out as objects for ridicule because they were handy and the royal governor and his superiors in England were not.

At first the abuse was only verbal. Because they wore red uniform coats the soldiers were called "lobsters" and "bloody backs," accompanied by obscene curses. Then the "far-outers" took to throwing ice and rocks at the sentries and guards as they paced their posts. The British soldiers could only mutter replies to the verbal abuse hurled at them. They could not return the physical barrages with anything at all short of firing upon their attackers, and they were under strict orders not to do so.

By March 5, 1770, the tension had built up to an explosive point. Snow had fallen that day over a ground covering of ice. About eight in the evening a British army captain named Goldfinch was crossing King Street, near where a sentinel was posted at the Custom House. Just then a barber's young helper hooted out (with appropriate insults) that Goldfinch still owed his master money for services rendered.

Hearing the abuse, the sentry chased the boy down the street, striking him several times with his musket butt. The boy was more scared than hurt, but his yells could be heard all over the neighborhood.

Then it was ominously quiet for a little while. Soon, however, an angry crowd gathered around the sentry. Shouting "Kill him! Kill the coward!" they pelted him with chunks of wood and sharp, heavy pieces of ice. The sentinel hollered for help and seven soldiers and one officer, Captain Preston, came running from the nearby barracks. The captain ordered his seven, plus the one on duty, to load their guns.

Ranged against the nine Britishers was a crowd of about a hundred ready to commit mayhem. They screamed curses, threw anything that could serve as a missile, and moved closer and closer. The soldiers, their weapons loaded, did nothing.

Then one of the troops was knocked off his feet by a hurled object. His gun went off—and the other soldiers, thinking that Preston had ordered them to shoot, fired away at the assembled mob. The result: three Bostonians dead, two others critically wounded and soon to die.

[43]

At once it seemed every Boston resident was out in the streets. The clamor did not die down until three the next morning, when Governor Hutchinson ordered an official inquiry that same day. Captain Preston and the eight soldiers were jailed, as much for their own safety as for the investigation to come. The governor's staff, the "crown men," feared the wrath of the colonists.

So did the crown attorneys. They were so frightened, in fact, that they would not defend Preston and the other eight on the charge of murder that was soon leveled against them. All the crown lawyers refused the assignment.

Who then would act for the jailed soldiers? Their friends scoured Boston in search of an advocate brave enough to stand against mob sentiment.

In time they reached John Adams. Whatever his personal feelings were about the charges, Adams also felt right down to the marrow of his bones that every man accused was entitled to a trial by jury and that the man was innocent until proved guilty. This was English law, the law that the colonists demanded for themselves. How could they deny it to the soldiers?

John Adams accepted the responsibility for defending the redcoats. His law partner, Josiah Quincy, Jr., volunteered to assist him. At once the prosecuting attorneys gathered depositions—sworn statements of fact—from ninety-six witnesses. Virtually all of them accused the soldiers of shooting into the crowd without provocation, of coolly and wantonly committing murder.

It was the task of Adams and Quincy to build an adequate defense, complete with their own witnesses, against these accusations. They could not deny that shots had been

Paul Revere made this engraving of the Boston Massacre as a propaganda poster, whipping up feeling against the British soldiers who fired on their colonial foes. The truth was somewhat different from this portrayal. COURTESY, THE BOSTONIAN SOCIETY, OLD STATE HOUSE

fired and men slain. They had to prove that the shootings were at least unavoidable.

Trial was scheduled for October, 1770. Preston was to be tried first, then the eight soldiers as a group. At Captain Preston's trial, the bombastic prosecuting attorney attempted to paint a picture of the man as a bloodthirsty commanding officer ready to kill on the slightest pretext. The lawyer triumphantly presented the depositions of the ninety-six witnesses as positive proof of his charges.

But Adams and Quincy produced witnesses of their own who swore that Preston was a peaceable man. Moreover, the jury simply would not accept the prosecution's wildly exaggerated case. They chose instead to believe the account of the defense, and brought in a verdict of "Not guilty."

Next came the trial of the enlisted men. A new jury was chosen, the judges seated. As in the Preston trial, the prosecuting attorney had to prove that the soldiers, without provocation, fired into the crowd because they were fundamentally cruel and evil. He attempted to do so in a torrent of words, but his defeat in the Preston case had somehow drawn the fire out of him.

Then John Adams had his turn to present the case for the defense. Slowly, carefully, drawing upon English law at every step to back his argument, he showed that there *was* provocation, that the soldiers were pushed beyond human endurance, that they had to fire to defend their own lives. He closed with a sober and reasonable plea:

Facts are stubborn things. And whatever may be our wishes, our inclinations, or the dictates of our passion, they cannot alter the state of facts and evidence. Nor is the law less stable than the fact. The law, in all vicissitudes of gov-

ernment, fluctuations of the passions, or flights of enthusiasm, will preserve a steady, undeviating course; it will not bend to the uncertain wishes, imaginations, and wanton tempers of men. To use the words of . . . Algernon Sidney: 'The law no passion can disturb. 'Tis void of desire and fear, lust and anger. 'Tis written reason, retaining some measure of the divine perfection. It commands that which is good and punishes evil in all, whether rich or poor, high or low. 'Tis deaf, inexorable, inflexible.'

JOHN ADAMS

. . . The law on the one hand is inexorable to the cries and lamentations of the prisoners. On the other it is deaf, deaf as an adder to the clamors of the populace. . . . Gentlemen, to your candor and justice I submit the prisoners and their cause.

John Adams was not fighting primarily for the lives or liberty of the soldiers. He was fighting for justice, for law, for the rule of right and reason in government and society. Justice and law won out—and so did the soldiers. Six were judged innocent. Two were judged guilty of manslaughter; their only penalty was to be branded on the thumb with a hot iron. The punishment was inflicted immediately. Then all walked out of the courtroom as free men.

In one important sense it was a personal victory for John Adams. In another equally important sense it was a victory for the whole colonial American cause—even though the defendants in this particular case were English. For the colonial struggle was a fight for law and justice, for the rights of free-born Englishmen everywhere, not only for those who lived in the island kingdom. It was this struggle which was to result in revolution, a revolution which would start only five years after the Boston Massacre.

[47]

Artist Gilbert Stuart did a portrait from life of Abigail Adams, from which this engraving was made. Busy, bustling Abigail found it hard to sit still for the artist. NEW YORK PUBLIC LIBRARY

As the first United States minister to Britain, John Adams presents his credentials and respects to America's old enemy, King George III.
NEW YORK PUBLIC LIBRARY

And what of John Adams, portly, red-faced, balding John Adams? He had been a fighter for a long time, and he would go on fighting. Eldest son of another John Adams, he had been born in a staunchly patriotic home in Braintree, now Quincy, Massachusetts, in 1735. Young Johnny helped his farmer father with the chores, skated on the frozen creeks in the winter, watched the tall-masted ships anchor in the bay in summer. All through his growing-up, he aimed at becoming a minister.

JOHN ADAMS

By the time he was graduated from Harvard College he had abandoned the clerical goal, and he went off to teach in the town of Worcester, Massachusetts. After a year he also began reading law in the late afternoons in the office of James Putnam. In time he was admitted to the bar and returned to Braintree to open a law office.

Young Adams married Abigail Smith, who became his partner and adviser in all his enterprises. They had four children. One of them, John Quincy Adams, became the sixth President of the United States (1825-29), after serving as Secretary of State under President James Monroe (1817-25). (John Quincy's son, Charles Francis, was minister to Britain during the Civil War. And Charles Francis's son, Henry, wrote *The Education of Henry Adams,* an autobiographical classic. John Adams' virtues, it seems, passed down almost undiminished through several generations.)

After his eloquent and successful Boston Massacre defense, John Adams became more and more a public figure. In 1774, he was chosen as a delegate to the First Continental Congress. At this Philadelphia meeting Adams met with delegates from other colonies. They sized one another up, found that they could agree, and decided to work together for the good of

[49]

all. It was there that Adams encountered Patrick Henry and judged his worth.

The Second Continental Congress began its war-long session in 1775. That year the delegates listened to Henry's impassioned plea for unshackling Britain's hold on the colonies. At that meeting Adams spoke stoutly for George Washington's appointment as commander of the colonial army. And the next year, 1776, Adams worked with Thomas Jefferson on the blazing indictment of British wrong-doing called the Declaration of Independence.

In 1778 Adams became one of three American representatives in France, negotiating for France's aid in the colonial struggle. Soon he was in Holland, there to plead for loans to carry on the Revolution. Both countries, due partly to Adams' urging, furnished massive aid. And they were the only two countries to recognize the independence of the United States before the end of the war.

After the peace treaty with Britain was finally signed in 1783, Adams was appointed the first U.S. minister to that nation. But he could get nowhere with the British in making trade agreements and was happy to return home in 1788.

Adams became, under President George Washington, the first Vice-President of the United States. He served two terms, and was the author of the statement that the Vice-Presidency is "the most insignificant office that ever the invention of man contrived or his imagination conceived." Yet he was not so unhappy as that damning definition would indicate.

In 1797 Adams was elected President. Thomas Jefferson, who ran second in the race for the office, became Vice-President, as the U.S. Constitution then provided. Adams' one term in office proved stormy. He fought with his own

Federalist party, with Jefferson's Democratic-Republican party, with Congress, and with France, once the closest friend of the United States.

In his last year as President, Adams moved with his family into the brand-new White House in Washington. It stood in a sea of mud and was still so unfinished that Abigail Adams hung her wash to dry in the vast East Room of the Presidential mansion.

Jefferson was elected President in 1800. On Inaugural Day, March 4, 1801, Adams fled Washington early in the morning without waiting to see Jefferson sworn in as his successor. In time, however, he and Jefferson put aside their quarrel and wrote to each other often and at length. Their correspondence makes fascinating reading. Both men died on July 4, 1826, fifty years to the day after the publication of the Declaration of Independence.

JOHN ADAMS

Adams, despite his sometimes hot temper, was one of the few logical and reasonable patriots on the Revolutionary scene. For him the law always preserved "a steady, undeviating course."

Sam Adams looks uncommonly neat in this portrait. Usually his clothes were shabby and his hair awry—he was too busy to pay attention to his appearance. NEW YORK PUBLIC LIBRARY

1773—"Boston Harbor
a teapot tonight!"

Agitation for American Independence had begun even before the matter of the writs of assistance that James Otis had attacked so strongly in 1761. The Stamp Act, even though it was unenforceable, added fuel to the fire —and Patrick Henry's eloquent speech against it in 1765 fanned the flames. The Boston Massacre, even though John Adams in 1770 ably defended the British soldiers involved in it, did the British no good in the end.

Even before the Boston Massacre another oppressive series of taxes had been levied on the colonies by Parliament. These came from the Townshend Acts, named for George III's new chancellor of the exchequer. The taxes were on paints, paper, glass, lead, and tea—all items the colonies had to import. The announced purpose of these taxes was to pay the salaries of the British colonial officials. Until now, their pay had come from appropriations made by the colonial legislatures. But the legislatures had an annoying habit of not voting the money whenever the officials proved especially unco-operative. Hence the new taxes.

The colonists, however, preferred to pay the officials— if they had to be paid at all—in the usual way. Their reaction to the new taxes was immediately to stop buying the taxed merchandise. Parliament was eventually forced to repeal most of the taxes (by coincidence, on March 5, 1770, the same day as the Boston Massacre). Only the tax on tea was retained.

Everybody, colonists and Britons alike, drank tea. It was the universal beverage, perhaps even more popular than coffee is in America today. The East India Company, a private enterprise chartered by and acting for the British govern-ment, had the sole right to sell tea both in England and the colonies. The East India Company's tea, brought in from India, Ceylon, and China, was expensive and heavily taxed. So both colonists and Britons bought smuggled—and untaxed—tea from the Dutch. The result, within a short time, was that the East India Company's warehouses be-came piled high with chests of unsold tea.

What to do with the overflowing accumulation of tea? The government devised what it considered an absolutely foolproof scheme. Parliament passed the Tea Act of 1773, giving the East India Company a complete monopoly on the sale of tea to the colonies. In addition, tea would be sold to the colonies only by the company's own agents, not by the tradesmen who once sold all teas, including the smuggled varieties.

The one factor that made the Tea Act seemingly fool-proof was that the East India Company's tea, including the tax, was priced even lower than the smuggled Dutch tea. What man in his right mind would pay more for smuggled tea when he could buy taxed tea for less?

The colonists, of course, liked the lower prices but they immediately resented the fact that the only tea they could buy came from the government. It was a restriction on the right to purchase what they wanted in a free market. It was tea this time. Next time it might be something even more necessary to existence—and the price could be anything Parliament wanted to make it. All this was imposed on the colonies by a legislature that had no colonial members in it, an increasingly sore point with the Americans.

Soon English ships bearing cargoes of legally-taxed tea dropped anchor in the harbors at New York, Philadelphia, and Portsmouth, Virginia. The Sons of Liberty, the bold and active patriots in each of these cities, forced the full-laden vessels to turn around and sail back to England.

Boston was next. The first tea ship, the *Dartmouth,* sailed into Boston Harbor on November 28, 1773, with 114 chests of tea in its holds. The *Dartmouth* was soon joined by the *Beaver* and the *Eleanor,* also carrying tea. The total cargo of the three vessels amounted to 342 chests of tea leaves.

For days the ships, moored to the wharves, tried to discharge their cargoes. The Boston patriots refused to let them do so. Thomas Hutchinson, the royal governor, ordered the harbor mouth guarded by cannon on land and frigates on the water, and refused to let the ships sail back with their cargoes still aboard.

On December 16, thousands of Bostonians crowded into

Old South Meeting House to hear impassioned speeches demanding that the full ships be sent back to England. At the frenzied high point of the session, a cold and decisive message came from Hutchinson: the ships must stay and be unloaded. At that news, the chairman of the gathering called out with dramatic finality: "This meeting can do nothing more to save the country!"

The chairman was Samuel Adams, whom historians have called "the Firebrand of the Revolution." With Adams' words came a rousing response from the gallery. But these were no ordinary cheers; they were Indian-style war whoops and other imitation-savage cries. And from the gallery descended a group of perhaps fifty men, blanket-wrapped, their faces smeared with dirt and lampblack, feathers in their hair. They certainly were not Indians, but their real identities were effectively disguised.

Adams gave them the signal to go. The "redskins" charged towards the wharves where the three ships were moored. On the way their ranks were swelled by a hundred more, and the cry went up: "Boston Harbor a teapot tonight!" Divided into three groups, they clambered aboard the three tea vessels.

It was all over in an incredibly short time. Warning the ships' crews not to interfere, the "Indians" hauled the tea chests up from the holds. With their Indian-type axes they ripped the covers from the chests, then dumped the loose tea leaves into the harbor's waters. The empty chests followed the tea overboard. Within three hours the task was done, and the "guests" at this Boston Tea Party bade one another a good goodnight. The floating leaves continued to lap against the sides of the ships for hours.

With the Boston Tea Party the American Revolution was one big step closer to becoming a reality. Although no one at the time could predict when the actual fighting would start, it was now almost exactly sixteen months away. And the man responsible for this Tea Party, and for many similar acts of defiance, was Samuel Adams.

Sam Adams was quite unlike his second cousin, sober, sensible John Adams, except that both were short and fat. Where John appealed to the people's reason, Sam appealed to their emotions. John tried to calm the people down, but Sam tried (and often succeeded) in stirring them up. Another nickname of his was "the Great Agitator."

Born in Boston in 1722, Sam Adams was the son of a prosperous brewer and member of the Caucus Club. This was an organization that advocated colonial self-government, and young Sam grew up hearing freedom talk all around him. At fourteen he entered Harvard College, where he studied mainly Greek and Latin.

Soon after graduation Sam got a loan of 1,000 pounds from his father to go into business for himself. And just as soon, he demonstrated a failing which was to pursue him throughout his lifetime—he was a poor businessman, careless about paying his bills and equally careless about collecting money owed him.

His own business declining, Sam Adams went to work in his father's brewery. At his father's death he inherited part of the estate. Young Adams soon spent his inheritance and was poor the rest of his days.

For a time he served as a tax collector, but he fell behind in his collections. After a while he completely gave up trying to earn a living by ordinary means and devoted himself to

[57]

politics. Such was the power of his political personality that his friends and supporters paid his bills, bought him clothes, built a barn for him and repaired his house. They took care of Sam Adams and his family in every way.

Despite the help of his friends, however, Adams' clothes continued to look shabby and his house rundown. His first wife died in 1757, leaving him with two children. He was married again seven years later to Elizabeth Wells, who cheerfully shared his poverty and his political activities.

When the Stamp Act was about to be imposed on the colonies, Sam Adams was the man chosen to write Boston's protest against the unjustified tax. In 1765 he was elected to the Massachusetts colonial legislature, where he served until 1774. As its clerk, he was in constant touch with the leaders of the other colonial legislatures. He fought hard against the Townshend Acts and helped see them abolished.

Sam Adams was probably one of the chief activists in the events that led to the Boston Massacre. It was here that he stepped over the line that divides legitimate protest from rabble-rousing. In fact he had a habit of inching over such divisions and getting himself into real trouble.

Adams was a good writer when aroused about an issue. He wrote many articles for the *Boston Gazette* and other papers. Adams was something of a political philosopher, too. In 1772 he made a motion in the Boston town meeting to appoint a "committee of correspondence . . . to state the rights of the colonists and of this province in particular, as men, as Christians, and as subjects. . . ." Named a member of that committee, Adams drafted a declaration of rights that foreshadowed the Declaration of Independence written four years later.

Sam Adams barely slipped by the Battle of Lexington on his way to the Continental Congress at Philadelphia. He may have even listened to the "shot heard round the world."

Adams' declaration begins: "Among the natural rights of the colonists are these: first a right to life; second, to liberty; third, to property; together with the right to support and defend them . . . These are . . . branches of . . . the first law of nature." After outlining natural rights, he went on to the rights of the colonists as Christians and as subjects of the king. He ended with a dire warning—or threat: "The colonists have been branded with the odious names of traitors and rebels only for complaining of their grievances." How long, Adams seemed to imply, would they stand for such treatment?

After the Boston Tea Party, Parliament retracted the Tea Act. In 1774, however, it imposed an even harsher penalty: the Intolerable Acts, as the colonists called them. The effect of this new law was to bottle up Boston Harbor, clamp down on town meetings, and force Bostonians to let British troops live in their homes.

Right then and there Sam Adams set up the hue and cry for armed revolt. He was elected to the First Continental Congress in 1774, and to the second congress that began meeting in 1775 and continued through most of the war. One of his fellow congressmen, Joseph Galloway of Pennsylvania, described Sam Adams as a man who "eats little, drinks little, sleeps little, thinks much, and is most decisive and indefatigable in the pursuit of his objectives."

Adams kept prodding and pushing for action until the first shots of the Revolution were fired at Lexington and Concord on April 18, 1775. Adams, on his way to congressional session in Philadelphia, was almost taken by the British at the Lexington engagement. A year later he was one of the proud signers of the Declaration of Independence.

Adams was active until the last. He served in the Continental Congress until 1781. He supported the new U.S. Constitution that emerged from the 1787 convention and helped secure its ratification by Massachusetts. In his old age he served as governor of Massachusetts, 1793-97. He died in 1803 in—to use his own phrase—"honorable poverty."

Even in old age Paul Revere was robust and hearty.

1775—"Listen my children and you shall hear..."

His name was Revere, Paul Revere, and he was a silversmith, a man who followed a sedentary, sit-down craft. But for all that, he was quick, strong, athletic, far more so than most men of forty. Above all, he was an excellent horseman, and it was as a mounted courier that he best served the cause of the Revolution.

Silversmith Revere, a member of the Boston chapter of the Sons of Liberty, sprang into action on the evening of April 18, 1775. A stable hand, overhearing two British soldiers, had come to him with vital news: British troops commanded by General Gage were marching on Concord that night to capture colonial stores of powder and shot. The British had another mission as well. Sam Adams and John

Hancock, two rebel leaders, were known to be at Lexington, near Concord, and Gage wanted to lay hands on them.

Revere sped through the streets carrying the news to Dr. Joseph Warren, who was in charge of the Sons of Liberty when Sam Adams was away. Warren had already been informed. Revere knew his next task was to warn the patriots along the way to Lexington and Concord that the British were on the march.

But first Revere had to learn from Dr. Warren which way the soldiers were proceeding. Would they go by land along the Neck which connected Boston to the mainland? Or would they take boats to Cambridge, then march on to Lexington and Concord? He needed to know this in order to signal the Charlestown militia of their approach. The signal would be to hang one lantern or two in the tower of Christ Church—one if the British were arriving by land, two if by sea.

"Hang two lanterns," the doctor told Revere. Warren also told him that he was dispatching William Dawes along an alternate route to warn the countryside that the British were near. Two riders doubled the chance that the message would get through.

Leaving Warren's house, Revere slipped quietly to Christ Church. There he instructed the sexton to hang two lanterns in the tower. Soon he was at the harbor where a boat with two oarsmen was waiting for him. Dipping their oars silently into the chill waters of Boston Harbor, the men rowed him across to Charlestown. The British warship *Somerset* lay at anchor in the black water, and nobody aboard noticed the little rowboat moving past in the still darkness.

At the Charlestown shore a horse, also arranged for, was

This unknown artist shows a full moon illuminating Paul Revere's famous ride. Moonlit or not, the ride has been known to every generation since Longfellow wrote his poem more than a century ago.

ready. Leaping into the saddle, Revere sped off into the night. Almost at once he was pursued by two British mounted troopers. Revere shook them off by jumping his steed over a wall and galloping down a stretch of farmland.

Passing through Medford, he awakened the sleeping town and saw the defenders at their posts. By midnight he was in Lexington, rousing the local militia and sending word to Adams and Hancock that the British were out to capture them. (All this can be found in a somewhat garbled version in Henry Wadsworth Longfellow's charming verse, *The Midnight Ride of Paul Revere,* with its opening line: "Listen, my children, and you shall hear/Of the midnight ride of Paul Revere.")

In Lexington, William Dawes rode up to join Revere. Dawes had been stopped by British sentries at the Neck, but his seemingly innocent face and plausible story that he was just passing by had won his release. Another young patriot, Dr. Samuel Prescott, came along to make a third member of the warning party. The three raced on towards Concord. However, British redcoats soon blocked their way. Prescott slipped through their grasp and rode ahead to warn the Minutemen, as the Concord patriots were called for their ability to hurry into a fight.

The British held Revere and Dawes for a time, then turned them free without their horses. The two hustled back to Lexington on foot. They arrived just in time to see Adams and Hancock depart for Philadelphia to attend the opening session of the Second Continental Congress.

Soon the main British force was at Lexington. They were able to scatter the militia defense, but their quarry—Adams and Hancock—were already safely on their way to Philadel-

phia. The redcoats then marched on to Concord. The Minutemen were ready for them at Concord Bridge. Poet Ralph
Waldo Emerson, sixty years later, summed up the meaning
of the skirmish in memorable lines: "Here the embattled
farmers stood/And fired the shot heard round the world."

These Minutemen were engaging in the opening round
of the Revolution itself—the conflict that had been building
up for years. All the hidden maneuvers and movements (such
as Revere had been involved in) were over. At last the
struggle was out in the open. It was to be fought on American
soil, but its impact was to be felt "round the world."

This was not to say, however, that all the colonists supported the war effort. Many stayed carefully neutral, hoping
later to join the side that seemed assured of victory. Many
others were openly loyal to king and Parliment. The patriots
numbered far less than a majority, and a large contingent
of these faltered before the war was won.

What was more, at this time even the patriots did not
consider it a war of *independence*, only a war to assert their
just claims against the British government. More than a year of
fighting would pass before Americans would claim their
freedom. Here, for example, is what Dr. Joseph Warren
wrote to his fellow citizens of Massachusetts a week after
Lexington and Concord. Describing what the redcoats did
as they retreated to Charlestown, he said:

*These, brethren, are the marks of ministerial vengeance
against this colony for refusing, with her sister colonies,
a submission to slavery; but they have not yet detached us
from our royal sovereign. We profess to be his loyal and
dutiful subjects, and, so hardly dealt with as we have been,
are still ready, with our lives and fortunes, to defend his*

[67]

At Lexington the massed British forces cut down the militia defense with a withering hail of musket fire. NEW YORK PUBLIC LIBRARY

The tranquility of a Massachusetts town was interrupted—and the Revolutionary War begun—at Concord, where the British suffered one of their first defeats. NEW YORK PUBLIC LIBRARY

person, family, Crown, and dignity. Nevertheless, to the persecution and tyranny of his cruel Ministry we will not tamely submit—appealing to Heaven for the justice of our cause, we determine to die or be free.

The freedom Dr. Warren was pleading for was not complete independence, not yet, at any rate. At this time he was only asking for the freedom granted other British subjects who lived on the home islands.

But Paul Revere was always a man for independence. He was an American who loved his country long before it became a nation, and he served it well in war and peace. Perhaps his love of country came from the fact that he was a member of a religious minority. His father, Apollos de Rívoire, was a French Huguenot, a Protestant in France where most of the people were Roman Catholic. Huguenots in France were not always openly persecuted, but they certainly felt the effects of discrimination.

Apollos came to America in 1716, looking for a more tolerant land in which to practice silversmithing. He settled in Boston and simplified the spelling of his last name to "Revere." Paul was born in 1735, a New Year's Day baby.

Boston, then as now, was a fine place to grow up in. The boy liked to go down to the shipyards to see the colonial vessels being built. He would cross over to the wharves to see the British merchant ships discharge their cargoes of English manufactured goods and take on new ones of Yankee raw materials. Paul went to school long enough to learn reading, writing, and arithmetic, enough for his needs as a future silversmith and businessman.

By the time he was thirteen Paul was an apprentice silversmith in his father's shop. He learned quickly, and when his

PAUL REVERE

father died nineteen-year-old Paul took over the business. Tom, his younger brother, had already started as an apprentice in the shop.

But Revere was always restless. He liked silversmithing, but he liked being out and about as well. At twenty-one, when the French and Indian War broke out, he enlisted for a year in the Massachusetts militia, leaving Tom in charge of the shop. During that year the only action he saw was against the French in upper New York. He came home, settled down to business, and married Sara Orne. They had eight children. (Sara died in 1773, and Revere married Rachel Walker. They had another eight offspring. Many of the children of both marriages died young, a commonplace occurence in those years.)

Even with a wife, family, and growing business, Paul Revere had time for outside interests. He joined Sam Adams' Caucus Club and heard the hubbub of talk about American freedom—and how Americans might someday have to fight for it. Sam Adams led the Boston protests against the Stamp Act, and Paul Revere was right behind him. Adams was active in inciting the Boston Massacre, and Revere made an engraving of the scene called "The Bloody Work on King Street." It showed the British soldiers as outright murderers, a highly inaccurate depiction but one that was very popular with the Bostonians. During the Boston Tea Party episode Revere kept the people outside the city informed and excited.

Revere was a man of many skills. He was an expert engraver of such pictures as the massacre scene. When the call for his silverwares died down, he taught himself how to make false teeth, cutting the teeth of sheep to fit the human mouth.

When the new United States declared its independence in 1776, he engraved the copper plates that printed the first U.S. paper money. He laid out a gunpowder factory during the Revolution and built a foundry that cast the first cannon ever made in America. He served as a colonel in the local militia.

When Revere died at eighty-three, church bells which had been cast in his foundry tolled in his memory.

*George Washington was warmer and gentler than this stern Gilbert
Stuart portrait would indicate.* NEW YORK PUBLIC LIBRARY

1775—"...a kind of destiny..."

Philadelphia, 18 June, 1775

My dearest,

    I am now set down to write you on a subject, which fills me with inexpressible concern . . . when I reflect upon the uneasiness which I know it will give you. It has been determined in Congress, that the whole army raised for the defense of the American cause shall be put under my care, and that it is necessary for me to proceed immediately to Boston to take upon me the command of it.

    . . . But as it has been a kind of destiny, that has thrown upon me this service, I shall hope that my undertaking it is designed to answer some good purpose. . .

That was George Washington writing to his wife, Martha. Four days before, at a stormy session of the Second Continental Congress, John Adams of Massachusetts had named George Washington of Virginia as a candidate for the post of commander-in-chief of the forces assembled to fight for America's cause. The next day Washington was chosen unanimously.

Tall, broad-shouldered, pockmarked George Washington, colonel in the Virginia militia, wealthy planter, was to become America's first (and still one of its greatest) heroes. But in the dark days of 1775, and in the darker days to come, Washington did not know whether his "kind of destiny" would lead to defeat and disgrace or to immortal glory.

Washington took over a force of about 15,000 men near Boston on July 3, 1775. Thereafter he was both commander of an army in the field and chief of the over-all effort against the British.

From the first, Washington suffered from many shortages and restrictions. The chief one perhaps was that the public lagged and wavered in its support of the war. Congress, under the Articles of Confederation, had no power to tax. It could only ask the state legislatures to furnish funds to carry on the war effort. These state governing bodies blew hot and cold when it came time to put up the money.

Congress also had to ask the states to furnish men. Again, the reluctant states were tardy in mustering troops. Washington was constantly plagued by a shortage of armed forces. He never had more that 20,000, all told, at any time, and most of these were bound to serve no more than six months or a year, no matter how long the war lasted. Against Washington were arrayed British regular soldiers, Loyalists (colonists who remained loyal to Britain), Indian allies, and mercenaries—hired soldiers, mainly Hessians from the German

*Washington was a vigorous, athletic man of forty-three when he took
command of the Continental army in 1775. He maintained that vigor
throughout the eight years of his command.* NEW YORK PUBLIC LIBRARY

Captain Nathan Hale stands tall as the British prepare to hang him for spying. LIBRARY OF CONGRESS

state of Hesse-Cassel and other small German principalities. These totaled at least 50,000.

The entire battle area was broad, from Quebec to Florida, from the Atlantic seaboard west to the Wabash River in what is now Indiana. America's Captain John Paul Jones even brought the sea attack to the English Channel. Washington, however, fought most of his battles in the Middle Atlantic area, mainly New York, New Jersey, and Pennsylvania. Only at the end of the fighting did he win the final and decisive victory in his home state of Virginia.

Washington's strategy was to send men out on a swift raiding attack, then pull back. He rarely had enough men and arms to risk a direct fight with the British, and always he had a problem of communication. The only way that word could be passed from army to army—or from squad to squad—was by messenger on foot or on horseback. This meant that most action, on a large scale, was sluggish.

For more than a year after he became commander of the American forces, Washington led his army in a series of feints and maneuvers with little direct contact with the British. Then the pattern of warfare changed.

August of 1776 found Washington on Long Island, New York, where his men were thrown into conflict with the forces of General Howe. The British onslaught drove the Americans to defense positions on the East River that divides Long Island from Manhattan. While Howe waited to attack again, the Americans crossed the river to Manhattan, steadily retreating. (It was during this engagement that the British captured the young American spy, Captain Nathan Hale, and executed him. Hale's classic farewell was patriotism at its loftiest: "I only regret that I have but one life to lose for my country.")

[77]

At White Plains, New York, north of Manhattan, Washington dug in and put up a fight. He had to retreat, however, holing up behind the Delaware River in New Jersey. In December's bitter cold he and his men sprang to the attack. Hessian troops were stationed at Trenton, New Jersey. Americans crossed the icy Delaware in small boats on the night of December 25-26, 1776, surprising the Hessians at their drunken Christmas Night revelry.

Britain's Lord Cornwallis then marched to defend Trenton. Washington slipped around the British defenses and sped on to Princeton, New Jersey. There, on January 3, 1777, he scored a smashing triumph, but could not follow it up. Instead he retreated to winter quarters at Morristown, New Jersey.

It was not until the following September that Washington again confronted the British. With arms furnished by France, now the secret ally of the young United States, Washington attacked at Brandywine Creek, southwest of Philadelphia. Despite their new arms, the Americans were unable to stop the British, who went on to take Philadelphia. Nor did a similar engagement a few weeks later at Germantown (now a part of Philadelphia) result in any American success.

Winter came early that year. Washington chose Valley Forge, twenty-five or so miles west of Philadelphia, as his winter retreat. The men straggled into the makeshift camp, a good half of them without footgear of any kind, their clothes, blankets, and tents tattered and worn. There was little food or other supplies for them. It was a hard season to bear.

Washington was especially bitter because he could not get the American government to feed his starving men. Martha Washington came to stay with him for a few weeks in Feb-

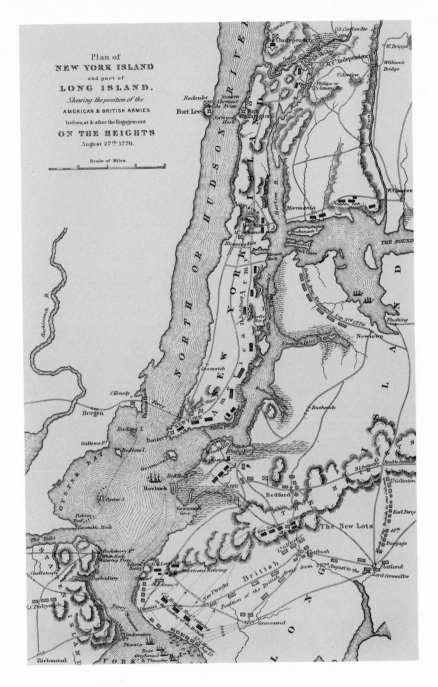

This map shows the battle lines at the Battle of Brooklyn Heights on August 27, 1776. It was one of the engagements from which Washington was forced to retreat and regroup his forces. NEW YORK PUBLIC LIBRARY

Critics of this famous painting of Washington crossing the Delaware claim that the boat would have tipped over long before the river was crossed. Seaworthy or not, the boat with its passengers has long been a symbol of American pride and patriotism. NEW YORK PUBLIC LIBRARY

ruary, 1778, comforting him a little during the bleak days. Washington was heartened too by the presence of his young French aide, the Marquis de Lafayette, who did much to brighten his commander's spirit.

Valley Forge represented the low point in the American war effort. As 1778 rolled on, France entered the war on the United States' side and the American prospect for victory improved.

It was not until 1781, however, that Washington, with French help, was able to tighten the pincers on the British and win the last and greatest victory. That year Britain's Lord Cornwallis, in command of a considerable segment of his country's army, established himself at Yorktown, Virginia. In a kind of classic chess maneuver, a French fleet of twenty-four ships commanded by Admiral François de Grasse sailed into Chesapeake Bay. Other French vessels moved into the mouth of the bay, sealing it off. French troops in the area put themselves under Washington's command, giving him a total of about 17,000 men.

Then the combined American and French land and sea forces moved in. They surrounded Cornwallis at Yorktown and laid siege. At the same time, de Grasse's fleet blocked British ships coming to help Cornwallis. It was weeks, however, before he gave up.

Finally, on October 19, 1781, Cornwallis's deputy turned over his sword to Major General Benjamin Lincoln, acting for Washington. As the surrender took place, the British band played a dolefully appropriate tune: "The World Turned Upside Down."

The fighting was virtually over, but the peace treaty was not signed for another two years. Not until November 25,

[81]

The Battle of Germantown, just outside Philadelphia, signaled an American retreat in the fall of 1777. NEW YORK PUBLIC LIBRARY

At Valley Forge the American forces were exhausted, dispirited, and without food, clothes, or weapons. Washington did his best to sustain the morale of his troops, but he had little cooperation from the Continental Congress. NEW YORK PUBLIC LIBRARY

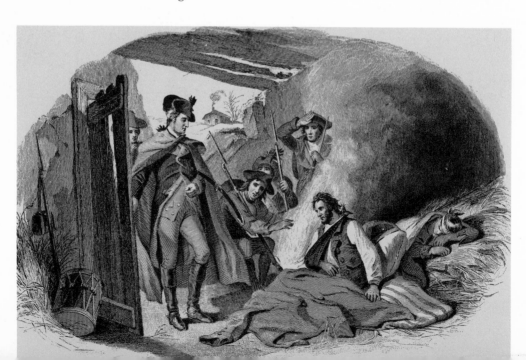

This engraving is a fictional account of the surrender of Cornwallis to Washington. In reality, neither general was present at the formal surrender, and the entire proceeding was conducted by their deputies.

1783, did the last of the British troops sail from New York Harbor. Washington led his men into the city that the British had held for so long and there said goodbye to them. Soon he was on his Mount Vernon plantation. There he hoped to spend the rest of his days as a working farmer. He was fifty-one years old.

Washington had earned an honorable retirement. He had led his country's armed forces to victory over a vastly superior army in the field, a victory forced upon an apathetic and sometimes sullen and uncooperative public at home. He was entitled to a rest.

Washington's "kind of destiny" began perhaps with a long-ago ancestor, great-grandfather John Washington, the first of the family in the New World. John settled in Virginia's Westmoreland County in 1657 on a grant of 150 acres alongside the Potomac River. Seventeen years later he received a grant of 5,000 acres some eighteen miles south of what is now Washington, D.C. This land would one day be known as Mount Vernon.

John's grandson Augustine was a bustling, energetic, enterprising man who expanded on his grandfather's holdings and launched business ventures as well. George, born February 22, 1732, was the eldest son of Augustine and his second wife, Mary Ball Washington. The boy had four older half-brothers and half-sisters and five younger brothers and sisters.

One of George Washington's nineteenth-century biographers, "Parson" Weems, made up many stories of George's boyhood—how he threw a stone clear across the Rappahannock River, how he chopped down the cherry tree and told his father. Weems had to concoct the stories, for little is known about Washington's early life.

At sixteen, his father dead, George was living with his half-brother Lawrence at Mount Vernon. Lord Fairfax, a neighbor and owner of more than 5,000,000 acres, employed George as a surveyor to assess his lands beyond the mountains. For more than a year the youth worked his way through timber and brush, charting the holdings of his land-rich master. When the work was complete George was appointed surveyor of Culpeper County. It was his first government post.

As the boy grew tall and strong, he took great pride in his appearance, his clothes, and the furnishings of his living quarters. He bought land and hunted and partied with his landed friends. It was a busy life, mainly in the outdoors, and the play was as strenuous as the work.

When Washington was twenty-one, the Virginia governor made him a major in the colonial militia and dispatched him with a protest message to the French who were building a line of forts across the Ohio country. It was Washington's first encounter with a rival people seeking possession of the North American continent. In 1754 Washington was in on the start of the French and Indian War when he and his Virginia militia company battled a French force near Fort Duquesne, on the site of present-day Pittsburgh, Pennsylvania. The Virginians were outnumbered, but eventually wormed their way free.

Next year a British general named Edward Braddock asked Washington to serve with him in an all-out campaign against the French-held Fort Duquesne. Washington accepted the assignment, but from the first he was appalled by Braddock's ignorance of the country and of the enemy. The general, despite Washington's warnings, insisted on fighting the French and Indians with his men advancing shoulder-to-shoulder as

[85]

During a pitched battle between the British on one side and the French and Indians on the other, Washington's chief, General Edward Braddock, was slain. NEW YORK PUBLIC LIBRARY

though on parade. The British were ripped apart and Braddock slain. Washington escaped unwounded, but reported that "I had four bullets through my coat and four horses shot under me. . ."

Washington had had enough of fighting for the time being. In 1759 he married Martha Dandridge Custis, a young widow with a small son and daughter. The Washingtons had no children of their own, but George was a generous and affectionate stepfather. He spent the next decade and a half in building up Mount Vernon and making it pay. He grew wheat and ground it in his own mills. He caught fish in the Potomac in commercial quantities and sold it, salted, by the barrelful. He grafted new fruit trees in his orchard and experimented with new field crops. He was a scientific farmer in an age when science was neither understood nor practiced.

Washington did not neglect his public duties. He remained a member of the Virginia legislature and a colonel in the militia. He was a magnificent host at parties and foxhunts. But war clouds gathered, and in 1775 he took command of the Revolutionary forces.

More than eight years passed before Washington could return to Mount Vernon. He found much to do to restore it to its former prosperity. For four more years he was an active—and careful—farmer. Then he was called again to public service.

This time he was asked to be chairman of the Constitutional Convention that assembled in Philadelphia during the summer of 1787. Delegates to the convention were pledged to revise the Articles of Confederation which had served as the nation's charter since the beginning of the war. But the pledge could not be honored, for the Articles could

[87]

Between the war and the presidency Washington was a working farmer at Mount Vernon. Martha is shown on the porch and their grandchildren are on the steps. NEW YORK PUBLIC LIBRARY

At Mount Vernon Washington owned slaves, as did his fellow planta-
tion owners. Long before his fellows did, however, Washington foresaw
the day when the slaves would be granted their freedom.

Mount Vernon sloped gently down to the broad Potomac River. Today,
countless visitors make their pilgrimage to this national shrine.

not be patched or repaired. Instead, the delegates wrote a brand-new Constitution that serves as the nation's legal framework today.

As with his Revolutionary command, Washington did not seek the convention's chairmanship. He did not refuse the responsibility, however, and he guided the convention's proceedings to a successful conclusion. Washington never pretended that he could tussle with such legal minds as James Madison and Alexander Hamilton, the convention's movers and shakers. Yet he had the rare ability to reduce a conflict to its debatable elements and help the contestants make a choice or come to a decision.

The Constitution was ratified, and it seemed logical that Washington become the nation's first President. He was inaugurated on April 30, 1789, in New York City, the temporary capital. His two-term administration was filled with "firsts"—the first census, the first ten amendments to the Constitution, the first toll road, and so on.

Washington faced crisis after crisis—and he lost his temper often. There was the time that the western Pennsylvania farmers refused to pay a tax on the whiskey they made from their own grain. They staged a "Whiskey Rebellion," and Washington immediately sent troops to enforce the tax laws. The farmers came round, Washington regained his composure, and the federal government proved for the first time that it was capable of enforcing one of its own laws.

Towards the close of his second term Washington offered his Farewell Address. Among other memorable statements in it is this one on international relations: "'Tis our true policy to steer clear of permanent alliances with any portion of the foreign world. . . . Taking care always to keep ourselves, by suitable establishments, on a respectable defensive posture, we may safely trust to temporary alliances for extraordinary emergencies. . . ." It is an admonition that modern American leaders are beginning to heed again.

On March 4, 1797, Washington turned over the Presidency to John Adams and returned to Mount Vernon once more. His last years were busy but brief. He died on December 14, 1799. In many ways he still is—recalling Richard Henry Lee's memorable phrase—"First in war, first in peace, first in the hearts of his countrymen."

GEORGE WASHINGTON

Red-haired, freckled Tom Jefferson was a man of great inner beauty and strength. NEW YORK PUBLIC LIBRARY

1776—"When, in the course of human events..."

Nights were hot in Philadelphia that late June of 1776. No cool breeze entered Thomas Jefferson's rented room on the second floor of a house at Seventh and Market Streets. Jefferson was laboring long and late on a paper that the Second Continental Congress had asked him to prepare. That paper was to be a blueprint for freedom.

Earlier that month, on June 7, Jefferson's fellow Virginia delegate, Richard Henry Lee had introduced a bold resolution before the Congress: "That these United Colonies are, and of right ought to be, free and independent states. . . ."

Lee's resolution was a challenge to the delegates from the other colonies. It was asking: Are you with us, or against us? Do you want independence, or do you want only to call off this fighting and return to the king's rule?

For the war which had begun more than thirteen months before was a *rebellion*—a protest against many kinds of unfair treatment. But it was not yet a *revolution*—a battle for freedom and independence, and many delegates to the Congress, on hearing the resolution, fought shy of it.

Some delegates were flatly against Lee's proposal. Some said they were not yet ready for it, for various reasons: The colonies were not well enough united; the colonies should first seek help from Britain's rival countries; the colonies should first listen to Britain's peace envoys, already said to be on their way; and so on.

Arguments over the resolution went on for days. Finally Edward Rutledge, a delegate from South Carolina who had fought the proposal, made a motion that voting on the resolution be put off until July 1. In the meantime, a committee was named to prepare a paper that would give the background and reasons for the controversial resolution. On the committee were Benjamin Franklin of Philadelphia, John Adams of Massachusetts, Roger Sherman of Connecticut, Robert Livingston of New York, and Thomas Jefferson of Virginia.

Franklin, seventy years old, was the elder statesman of the committee. Adams, forty-one, was well known for his outspoken advocacy of independence. Sherman, fifty-five, a country lawyer, asked shrewd questions. Livingston, young, wealthy, and conservative, backed away from the committee's radical direction. Then there was Tom Jefferson, thirty-three, tall, red-haired and quiet.

No speaker, Jefferson was good at working with small groups. And his range of talents was immense. A lawyer by vocation, he was also a linguist, scientist, musician, inventor,

Philadelphia during the summer of 1776 was a very active place, all
agog with revolutionary fervor. FREE LIBRARY OF PHILADELPHIA

Franklin, Jefferson, Adams, Livingston, and Sherman gather to discuss
—and approve—Jefferson's draft of the Declaration of Independence.
NEW YORK PUBLIC LIBRARY

By candlelight, Jefferson reads over his now-immortal Declaration. NEW YORK PUBLIC LIBRARY

architect, and curious about everything. Jefferson was asked to do the actual writing of the paper. He accepted reluctantly, then—as in everything else he undertook—he settled down to do his very best.

Summer had officially been on the calendar for several days when Jefferson completed his paper. He called it "A Declaration by the Representatives of the United States of America, in General Congress assembled." The world now knows it by its simpler title: "The Declaration of Independence."

THOMAS
JEFFERSON

Jefferson began his immortal declaration with a calm statement of his reasons for writing it:

When, in the course of human events, it becomes necessary for one people to dissolve the political bands which have connected them with another, and to assume, among the powers of the earth, the separate and equal station to which the laws of nature and of nature's God entitle them, a decent respect to the opinions of mankind requires that they should declare the causes that impel them to the separation.

Then he went on to lay the groundwork for the people's right to revolt:

We hold these truths to be self-evident, that all men are created equal, that they are endowed by their Creator with certain unalienable rights, that among these are life, liberty, and the pursuit of happiness. That to secure these rights, governments are instituted among men, deriving their just powers from the consent of the governed. That whenever any form of government becomes destructive of these ends, it is the right of the people to alter or abolish it. . .

[97]

A Declaration by the Representatives of the UNITED STATES OF AMERICA, in General Congress assembled.

When in the course of human events it becomes necessary for one people to dissolve the political bands which have connected them with another, and to assume among the powers of the earth the separate and equal station to which the laws of nature & of nature's god entitle them, a decent respect to the opinions of mankind requires that they should declare the causes which impel them to the separation.

We hold these truths to be self-evident; that all men are created equal; that they are endowed by their creator with equal rights, some of which are inherent & inalienable; among these are life, liberty, & the pursuit of happiness; that to secure these rights, governments are instituted among men, deriving their just powers from the consent of the governed; that whenever any form of government becomes destructive of these ends, it is the right of the people to alter or to abolish it, & to institute new government, laying it's foundation on such principles & organising it's powers in such form, as to them shall seem most likely to effect their safety & happiness. prudence indeed will dictate that governments long established should not be changed for light & transient causes: and accordingly all experience hath shewn that mankind are more disposed to suffer while evils are sufferable, than to right themselves by abolishing the forms to which they are accustomed. but when a long train of abuses & usurpations [begun at a distinguished period &] pursuing invariably the same object, evinces a design to reduce them under absolute Despotism, it is their right, it is their duty, to throw off such & to provide new guards for their future security. such has been the patient sufferance of these colonies; & such is now the necessity which constrains them to expunge their former systems of government. the history of the present king of Great Britain is a history of unremitting injuries and usurpations, [among which, appears no solitary fact] to contradict the uniform tenor of the rest but all have in direct object the establishment of an absolute tyranny over these states. to prove this, let facts be submitted to a candid world [for the truth of which we pledge a faith yet unsullied by falsehood.]

Jefferson's original draft of the Declaration of Independence shows a steady, driving development of thought and theme. LIBRARY OF CONGRESS

Jefferson's ideas were not new. Other men before him had said that kings have no divine mandate to rule as they please, that every man has God-given rights, that governments are to be controlled by the people they govern. But no one before Jefferson had been able to say it so well.

With this eloquent beginning Jefferson proceeded to list the "long train of abuses," the grievances that the king had inflicted on the colonists—unjust laws, unwarranted taxes, unfair trials, and a host of other charges. He recited the *THOMAS* steps the colonists had taken to protest these grievances, *JEFFERSON* peaceful pleas that had fallen on unheeding ears.

He concluded his paper with a ringing statement of resolute purpose: "And for the support of this declaration, with a firm reliance on the protection of Divine Providence, we mutually pledge to each other our lives, our fortunes, and our sacred honor."

Franklin and Adams read the draft with delight and enthusiasm, suggesting a few minor changes in wording. They vowed to fight for its adoption and for the continuing American struggle for freedom.

At 9 A.M. on Monday, July 1, 1776, John Hancock of Boston, president of the Congress, called the meeting to order in the Pennsylvania State House. The gloomy reports of military defeats and setbacks for the colonies took hours. It was a bad background for the debate over the declaration that was soon to begin.

Discussion of Jefferson's paper opened with an attack on it by John Dickinson of Pennsylvania. Dickinson was an old foe of independence, an old believer in loyalty to king and Parliament. He railed at the declaration, arguing that it would bring defeat by Britain and disgrace in the eyes of all Europe. He charged that the colonists would not stand behind it,

[99]

and would, indeed, consider the declaration an act of madness.

When Dickinson finished, the delegates were silent. Only John Adams rose to answer the attack. Starting slowly and deliberately, Adams reported the facts of the situation—how Britain had rejected the colonies' claims, how its armies were now overrunning the land. The time for reconciliation, for resuming the old relationship, was past.

Warming up, Adams called for such a declaration to win friends for America from the other European powers. It would, he said, crystallize support of the people in every colony behind the patriot cause. Adams ended his argument with a ringing cry of personal involvement: "All that I have, all that I am, and all that I hope for in this life, I am now ready to stake on this resolution. Live or die, survive or perish, I am for the declaration!"

When Adams sat down there was much confusion. A trial vote was taken: nine colonies were for the declaration. Pennsylvania and South Carolina were against it. Delaware's delegation had split its vote evenly, thus canceling it. New York abstained. The official vote was put off until the next day.

Then followed a day and a night of furious maneuvering. A missing Delaware delegate, Caesar Rodney, who was for the declaration, was found. South Carolina's Rutledge came round to seeing that his colony could not stand in the way of freedom. New York would continue to abstain. Pennsylvania's Dickinson dropped out of the voting, giving the pro-Declaration delegates from Pennsylvania a majority of one. (Although Dickinson never voted for the Declaration, he was one of the few delegates who actually fought in the Revolutionary army.)

The Old State House in Philadelphia soon had a
new name—"Independence Hall." NEW YORK PUBLIC LIBRARY

Representatives of the colonies voted 12-0 (with New York abstaining) in favor of the Declaration of Independence. NEW YORK PUBLIC LIBRARY

The vote on July 2 was twelve colonies for, one abstaining, none against. America was committed to fight for independence, and the words of that commitment, published on July 4, were Tom Jefferson's.

"I have sworn upon the altar of God eternal hostility against every form of tyranny over the mind of man." This was Jefferson's credo, and throughout his life he did his best to remain true to it. Born in 1743 and reared in the red hills of western Virginia, he began early to free his own mind from any sort of tyranny.

THOMAS JEFFERSON

As a boy he combined an outdoor life with serious studies in languages, mathematics, literature, and philosophy. For two years he was a student at William and Mary College, in Williamsburg, Virginia. Then he studied law under George Wythe (who later was one of the signers of the Declaration of Independence).

Jefferson entered politics as a member of the Virginia legislature and the Continental Congress, and later as wartime governor of Virginia. It was as a Virginia legislator that he was responsible for a statute preventing public law from controlling private belief. It was as a Congressman that he served as the principal writer of the Declaration of Independence.

Three years before he entered Congress he married Martha Wayles Skelton, a young widow. They had six children, only two of whom reached adulthood. Martha Jefferson did not survive the birth of her sixth child. Jefferson never remarried.

After his wife's death Jefferson again served in Congress and as minister to France. In 1790 he became the nation's first Secretary of State under George Washington. He filled this post until 1793, then retired—for good, he thought. He wanted more time to be with his children, to write, to read, to invent and experiment, to play his violin, to work on his beautiful Monticello house.

But in 1796 he was called back to politics. He was elected Vice-President under President John Adams, whom he increasingly opposed. Adams belonged to the Federalist party, and Jefferson was the leader of the new Democratic-Republican party (forerunner of the modern Democratic party). As political opponents and as members of opposing parties, Adams and Jefferson had little to say to each other.

In the election of 1800 Jefferson was his party's candidiate for President and Adams ran for reelection under the Federalist banner. Jefferson won by an electoral vote of seventy-three to sixty-three. There was another candidate, Aaron Burr, who had originally intended to run for President, but who then changed his mind and ran for Vice-President on Jefferson's ticket.

Burr, however, had failed to withdraw his Presidential candidacy. Thus when the Democratic-Republican electors cast their ballots for Jefferson and Burr, they were in effect electing two Presidents. It took more that thirty votes by the House of Representatives to resolve the mix-up. In 1804 Jefferson's reelection to a second term was almost unopposed.

Jefferson's hatred of tyranny over the mind of man led him to oppose "big," centralized government. He did not want all the laws and governing edicts to come from Washington, D.C. He wanted agriculture, not manufacturing, to be the economic mainstay of the country. He could not foresee that the United States would become the foremost industrial nation in the world.

Presidential inaugurations in Jefferson's day were casual. Here, President-elect Jefferson hitches up his horse before walking to the inaugural site. NEW YORK PUBLIC LIBRARY

Jefferson was his own architect, contractor, and construction superintendent for his lovely Monticello mansion in Virginia.

After his second term as President, Jefferson returned to Monticello, free at last from the responsibilities of public office. He began corresponding with John Adams, and they remained friends for the rest of their lives. He took the leadership in setting up the University of Virginia at Charlottesville, and engaged in a thousand other projects—literary, scientific, agricultural, architectural, musical. He was never idle, never bored.

Jefferson died on July 4, 1826, fifty years to the day after the publication of the Declaration of Independence. (Adams died on that same day.) On his tombstone Jefferson asked that these words be engraved:

Here was Buried
THOMAS JEFFERSON
Author of the
Declaration
of
American Independence
of the
Statute of Virginia
for
Religious Freedom
and Father of the
University of Virginia

He did not care to be remembered for his Presidency, nor for his many lesser elective and appointive offices. Of the three achievements he deemed important, the Declaration of Independence came first. The world today agrees with Tom Jefferson's choice.

Tom Paine, master pamphleteer and propagandist, looked ordinary—except for his burning eyes and determined jaw.

1776—"These are the times that try men's souls."

He was thirty-seven years old, not much to look at, poorly educated. In America for only two years, he was now serving a short-term enlistment in the Continental Army. But he was also a writer, a political writer, whose words inspired and inflamed the colonists as no other journalist or pamphleteer, speaker or preacher, could do. His name was Thomas Paine, and everybody called him "Tom."

In the late autumn of 1776, Washington's forces were beating a retreat from New York across New Jersey. Private Tom Paine, already known for his political pamphlet *Common Sense,* was traveling fast and light with his fellow soldiers. As he marched, the words of another pamphlet were already taking shape in his head. One night, by the flickering light of a campfire, he began to set his thoughts down on paper. The new pamphlet opened with these words:

These are the times that try men's souls. The summer soldier and the sunshine patriot will, in this crisis, shrink from the service of his country; but he that stands it now deserves the love and thanks of man and woman. Tyranny, like hell, is not easily conquered; yet we have this consolation with us—that the harder the conflict, the more glorious the triumph. What we obtain too cheap, we esteem too lightly: It is dearness only that gives everything its value. Heaven knows how to put a proper price on its goods; and it would be strange indeed if so celestial an article as freedom should not be highly rated. Britain, with an army to enforce her tyranny, has declared that she has a right not only to tax but 'to bind us in all cases whatsoever,' and if being bound in that manner is not slavery, then there is not such a thing as slavery upon the earth. . . .

Then Paine proceeded to a quick and accurate analysis of why Washington had retreated and why the British general, Howe, had failed to pursue the Americans. Praising Washington's leadership, he returned again and again to his plea for public support of the war effort. His language was strong and plain, his arguments powerful and logical:

I thank God that I fear not. I see no real cause for fear. I know our situation well, and can see the way out of it. While our army was collected, Howe dared not risk a battle; and it is no credit to him that he decamped from the White Plains [New York] and waited a mean opportunity to ravage the defenseless Jerseys. But it is great credit to us that, with a hand-

[110]

ful of men, we sustained an orderly retreat for near a hundred miles. . . . Once more we are again collected and collecting, our new army at both ends of the continent is recruiting fast, and we shall be able to open the next campaign with sixty thousand men, well armed and clothed. . . .

(Paine's estimate of 60,000 well-equipped soldiers was overly optimistic—Washington never had more than 20,000 to command, and most of these were without proper gear.)

The piece appeared in the *Pennsylvania Journal* on December 19, 1776, and four days later was reprinted as a pamphlet, the first issue of *The American Crisis* series of publications.

As soon as the article came out, it was read by, or read to, virtually every American soldier and most civilians. It heartened the people and united them around a cause that many had already begun to lose faith in. It brought many new enlistments in the Continental Army.

The American Crisis had its immediate results, too. The article did much to inspire the Americans under Washington when they attacked the Hessians at Trenton, New Jersey, on December 26, only a few days after the pamphlet's publication. The Americans demolished the Hessian forces, which suffered about nine-hundred casualties to the colonists' four.

Tom Paine was soon one of the most talked-about men in the colonies. Everyone recognized and admired his way with words, his sense of drama. But where did he get his fire, his passion, his ability to sway readers? His background gives few clues. Paine was born in 1737 at Thetford, England. His father was a poor Quaker corset maker, his mother the daughter of an attorney. Tom left school at thirteen and became an apprentice in the corset-making trade. At nineteen, when

Here General Washington accepts the surrender of Britain's Colonel Rall at Trenton. The American victory owed much to the inspiration provided by Tom Paine's American Crisis *pamphlet.* NEW YORK PUBLIC LIBRARY

This is the title page of Paine's Common Sense *pamphlet. Note that the printer, "R. Bell," is named here, but Paine is not.* LIBRARY OF CONGRESS

COMMON SENSE;

ADDRESSED TO THE

INHABITANTS

OF

AMERICA,

On the following interesting

SUBJECTS.

I. Of the Origin and Design of Government in general, with concise Remarks on the English Constitution.

II. Of Monarchy and Hereditary Succession.

III. Thoughts on the present State of American Affairs.

IV. Of the present Ability of America, with some miscellaneous Reflections.

Man knows no Master save creating HEAVEN,
Or those whom choice and common good ordain.
THOMSON.

PHILADELPHIA;

Printed, and Sold, by R. BELL, in Third-Street.

MDCCLXXVI.

the French and Indian War broke out, he went to sea aboard
a privateer (a privately owned ship acting as a naval vessel) .
But the life of a common sailor proved harsh and lonely.

For the next eighteen years Paine worked at a series of
ordinary jobs—corset maker, tax collector, school teacher,
shopkeeper. He was dissatisfied, but he was unable to find a
way out. At the same time, however, he took a keen interest
in science, mathematics, politics. He was educating himself in
subjects which had no practical use at the moment, but
which later would be of immense benefit.

Paine got his chance in 1772, when he served as representative for his fellow tax collectors who were petitioning
Parliament for more pay. For this he was fired. But it brought
him to the attention of Benjamin Franklin, then serving as
agent for the colonies in London. Franklin advised him to
make a new start in Philadelphia and gave him letters of
recommendation in which Paine was described as an "in-
genious, worthy young man."

Reaching Philadelphia on November 30, 1774, Paine was
soon supporting himself by writing for the *Pennsylvania
Magazine*. In a little while he became its editor. He wrote
articles on a wide variety of subjects, but his major interest
was politics. He soon sensed that many of the colonists wanted
relief from certain harsh British measures, principally unjust
taxes. But they were not yet thinking of independence.

From the first, however, Paine was a strong advocate of
American freedom. He wanted an end to rule by the king
and all that such a rule brought with it. And after Lexington
and Concord, he became a bold fighter for *all* men's freedom.
For example, he wanted the Continental Congress to do a
virtually unheard-of thing: he wanted it to stop the buying

and selling of Negro slaves, to make the lives of slaves easier, and in time to liberate them completely.

Six months before the Declaration of Independence was published, Paine launched his own arguments for American freedom. On January 10, 1776, he put out a forty-seven page pamphlet called *Common Sense* that sold for two shillings. In it he outlined his reasons for breaking away from Britain —that a continent could not stay tied to an island, that American freedom from a vicious king could set an example for the whole world.

In less than three months, 120,000 copies of *Common Sense* were sold, a total of a half million within a year or so—in a country where the first census (1790) counted a total population of about four million. Dr. Benjamin Rush, noted Philadelphia physician and signer of the Declaration of Independence, said the pamphlet had an effect "which has rarely been produced by types and paper in any age or country."

After *The American Crisis* came out, Paine served for a time as Secretary of the Committee of Foreign Affairs, a forerunner of the United States State Department. But he became involved in a controversy over how the French aid to America (secret at that time, because France was not yet ready to publicize its help) should be handled. He was forced to resign. He was soon appointed clerk to the Pennsylvania Assembly, and all the while he continued publishing further installments of the *Crisis*.

With the Revolution won, Paine settled down on a farm given him by New York State and further financed with a gift of $500 from Pennsylvania. Writing and working on the idea of a new type of bridge occupied him for several

Tom Paine died in poverty and neglect in 1809. Disinterested onlookers witnessed his last moments. NEW YORK PUBLIC LIBRARY

years. The bridge was to be of iron, not wood, and supported by an arch. But the revolutionary zeal was still strong in him, and when the French Revolution broke out in 1789 he was off to Paris at once.

For the next three years Paine shuttled between London and Paris, spreading the good word of the French Revolution, as he had of the American Revolution. Pamphlets were the best way to spread the word, and Paine's gift was for pamphleteering. So it was only natural that he would write *Rights of Man* in defense of the French uprising.

In *Rights of Man* Paine argued that government exists to guarantee a person those rights he cannot be sure to obtain by himself. These rights—and all men alike are entitled to them—are liberty, property, security, and resistance to persecution. Paine held that only a republican government could honestly offer these rights, and then only if that government had a written constitution which included a bill of rights, the vote, administrative officials elected for short terms, judges and courts that were in the end controlled by the voters, an elected legislature, and a public not legally divided by differences in birth or rank, religion, or money. Paine had learned his lessons well from the American Revolution.

But the French Revolution, which had executed its king as a tyrant, itself grew even more tyrannical. Paine was arrested and saved only by the U.S. minister to France, who vouched that Paine was an American citizen—which he still was. Released, he stayed in France for several years writing *The Age of Reason,* a defense of religion but an attack on organized creeds.

Paine spent the last seven years of his life in and near New York City. *The Age of Reason* had made him many new enemies, and his old friends had largely forgotten him. He died in 1809, and for years his achievements were either ignored or denied. President Theodore Roosevelt, usually a fair-minded man, called him a "filthy little atheist." But modern historians have set the record straight. Today the world recognizes Paine as a stout fighter for democracy, a great lover of his fellow man, and the world's best writer on revolutions.

A formal portrait of Lafayette. In his later years he regarded his American adventures as the most glorious episodes in his career. NEW YORK PUBLIC LIBRARY

1777—"Not to teach
but to learn..."

When people think of a revolution, they think of the oppressed poor casting off their shackles and rising against their rich and well-born masters, as in the French Revolution of 1789 and the Russian Revolution of 1917. These struggles were generally between the "haves" and the "have-nots," with the latter winning—and taking over.

The American Revolution did not fall into that pattern, however. There were several differences. For one, the Americans were fighting only for the same rights as native-born Englishmen already enjoyed—self-rule under a representative government. The Americans wanted the same freedom as people in Britain already had.

Another difference was that the British did not stand for the "haves" and the Americans for the "have-nots." Many of the American leaders were nearly as wealthy and aristocratic as their counterparts in Britain. A large number of the ordinary American soldiers were, in civilian life, men who owned their own farms or businesses. On the other hand, many of the British soldiers were drafted from the city slums or from the families of tenant farmers or workers on the great estates. And many of the units in the British regiments were Hessians—hired soldiers (mercenaries) from the small German principalities.

So it was no great wonder that a high-ranking young French nobleman, and rich to boot, chose to serve the American cause. He was filled with a love of freedom and a hatred for Britain, the nation that had defeated his own country in the Seven Years War. The young man was Marie Joseph Paul Yves Roch Gilbert du Motier, Marquis de Lafayette, known to his associates and to history as Lafayette. He was not yet twenty when he reported to Washington in August 1777. The French government had pulled the strings of the Continental Congress to obtain an appointment as major general for Lafayette, even though he lacked any battle experience.

Washington objected to the appointment on general principles, saying that other French volunteers had seemed modest at first but soon demanded posts they had "no right to look for." However, Washington took to this latest French volunteer. Lafayette was getting bald in front; his face was thin; his nose was long and pointed; and his chin jutted out. His slim body tightened with his effort to succeed as a soldier. And, of all things, he was soon working hard to learn English, something few continental Europeans ever bothered to do.

Although Lafayette had never led soldiers in actual fighting, he did have long years of schooling as an officer in several French regiments. Soon after he arrived in Philadelphia, Washington said to him, "We . . . feel embarrassed to exhibit ourselves before an officer who has just quitted French troops."

Replied Lafayette, "It is not to teach but to learn that I came hither."

The Frenchman had always been a good student. He was born in 1757 in the huge, gloomy castle of Chavaniac, located in the province of Auvergne, France. Only two years later his father, Gilbert, Marquis de Lafayette, was slain fighting at Minden, one of the battles of the Seven Years War (1756-63). The boy, also called Gilbert, inherited the title of marquis.

At the castle Gilbert lived with his grandmother, two old aunts, and a priest who served as his tutor. His mother, now a widow, preferred the gaiety of her father's magnificent home in Paris to the gloom of Chavaniac. Her father, in contrast to her husband's family, was rich. He let Gilbert's mother spend his money as long as she stayed in Paris, but gave her little to send to Chavaniac.

When he was eleven Gilbert was enrolled in the Collège du Plessis, a boarding school. But only two years later his mother and his grandfather both died. Now, in addition to his father's title he had his grandfather's fortune, an annual income of 120,000 *livres* (a *livre* was worth about nineteen cents in American money). Suddenly he had became one of the richest noblemen in France.

Money or no, the boy was determined to follow a military career. Still in his early teens, he became a junior officer in the King's Musketeers. And before he reached the age of seventeen he was married. It was an arranged match, a common practice in those days when it was believed that young people did not have sense enough to choose proper mates for themselves. Gilbert's bride was two years younger than he.

She was Adrienne d'Ayen, daughter of the Duc d'Ayen and granddaughter of the Maréchal de Noailles, one of the most powerful men in the French royal government.

Even though it was an arranged marriage, Gilbert and Adrienne soon grew to love each other. It was expected that the young Lafayettes would spend much time in the social whirl of Queen Marie Antoinette's court. But Gilbert danced badly and had no head or stomach for liquor. Nor did Adrienne fit in much better. They were glad to leave the court whenever they could for the clearer air of army life.

In the summer of 1775 Lafayette attended a dinner in honor of the Duke of Gloucester. The Duke, even though he was English, spoke sympathetically about the American cause. This was the first time that Lafayette had ever heard the American side of the story. He was moved and shaken.

During the weeks and months that followed, Lafayette saw his future taking shape. If he went to America to help the rebels he would be accomplishing a twin purpose: he would strike back at Britain for defeating the French in the Seven Years War—and he would be avenging his father's death in that war. He would do it, he vowed. And there would be only *la gloire*—the glory—in store for him.

After the Declaration of Independence was published on July 4, 1776, Lafayette began dealing with Silas Deane and Arthur Lee, the American commissioners in Paris. Over the next several months they worked out an agreement under which Lafayette would serve without pay if he were granted an officer's commission in the American armed forces. He bought a ship, *La Victoire,* and set sail for the New World.

Even though it meant leaving Adrienne and their infant daughter, Lafayette was jubilant. His excitement did not

Washington, somewhat withdrawn, meets his ardent French volunteer, Lafay-ette. LIBRARY OF CONGRESS

Lafayette speaks to his French well-wishers before boarding boat that will take him to his ship, La Victoire. *Its destination: revolution-torn America.*
NEW YORK PUBLIC LIBRARY

lessen during the seven weeks' voyage. It continued through the complicated dealings with Congress that eventually won him his commission and his chance to serve.

Lafayette saw his first action at the Battle of Brandywine, outside Philadelphia, in September, 1777. There the British routed the colonial forces, but Lafayette held his troops in line long enough to permit the rest of the army to fall back without major casualties. During the battle Lafayette was wounded in the leg. He refused to be treated until all his men had taken cover. Not until Washington himself ordered him to leave did he take cover himself.

Washington told the doctors, "Treat him as though he were my own son." And Washington meant it. The American commander had no son of his own (he had a stepson, Jackie Custis, son of his wife by her first husband), and he needed someone he could trust. Lafayette wrote his wife that Washington "finds in me a sincere friend, in whose bosom he may always confide his most secret thoughts, and who will always speak the truth." The deep regard that each man had for the other never wavered.

Lafayette spent a month recuperating from his wound, then rejoined Washington. That winter, the darkest winter of the war, the main body of American forces retreated to a camp at Valley Forge, Pennsylvania. Washington moved his headquarters to the winter camp, and Lafayette stayed by his side. By this time Lafayette commanded the Virginia Division, and the Frenchman did much to relieve the poverty and hardship of his men at Valley Forge. He bought them food, clothing, shoes with his own money.

At the same time Lafayette was learning the art of leadership. He wrote his father-in-law, the Duc d'Ayen:

I read, study, listen, and think, and while turning all this
over in my mind, I try to formulate an over-all view of things
that will remain true to common sense. I try not to say
very much, in order not to say anything foolish—and I shall
try to be very cautious in order not to do anything foolish. . . .
I do not believe that the desire for success and la gloire *should*
threaten the safety of a whole army.

It was this threat to the army's safety that prompted Lafayette to act in what became known as the Conway Cabal. This was a plot to overthrow the leadership of General Washington, a plot undertaken by two leading generals. One was General Horatio Gates, hero of the Battle of Saratoga, a victory which ended the American string of defeats. The other was General Thomas Conway, an Irish-born and French-trained commander of American troops.

One of their first moves was to try to turn Lafayette away from Washington. They tried to invite him to their quarters at York, Pennsylvania. But Lafayette would not leave Valley Forge. They then came to Valley Forge and urged Lafayette to quit and go home while he still had a good reputation. Otherwise, Conway suggested, he would go down to defeat and disgrace along with Washington.

Lafayette at first refused to recognize what Conway and Gates were trying to do. Then he saw letters between the two that made their intentions clear. He wrote Washington, telling his leader of the plot. Washington wrote back, saying, "We must not, in so great a contest, expect to meet with nothing but sunshine. I have no doubt that everything happens for the best, that we shall triumph over all our misfortunes, and in the end be happy."

In January, 1778, the Gates-Conway forces tried a complex scheme to separate Lafayette from Washington. They succeeded in getting Congress to authorize an American expedition to Canada and to put Lafayette in charge of it. Lafayette accepted the assignment, but made it clear that he was still taking orders from Washington. Britain had taken Canada as the major prize in its victory in the Seven Years War, called in America the French and Indian War, and Lafayette saw his chance to recapture Canada and give it back to France.

Lafayette at once journeyed to Albany, New York, ready to take command of the 3,000 well-equipped men promised him for the expedition. He found only 1,200 soldiers. These were as hungry, poorly clad, and poorly armed as those he had left behind at Valley Forge. And there he found General Conway himself, full of hints that this was all Washington's fault. Lafayette soon realized that he had been tricked, not by Washington, but by forces that were trying to destroy Washington. He again informed his chief of Conway's schemes. By this time Conway was completely discredited—and Lafayette and Washington were closer than ever.

In the spring of 1778 Lafayette returned to Valley Forge. Soon the American forces heard great news. The French king, Louis XVI, had signed a treaty of alliance with the United States. It meant that French aid would no more be handed out secretly; France would instead openly help America in its fight for freedom. Lafayette was immensely proud when Washington told him how much he had done to bring about this great event.

That summer Lafayette took part in several campaigns, notably in one in which the English attempted to kidnap him and send him back to Paris to be laughed at. Lafayette was already planning to make a visit home, but he did not

The British laid siege to Charleston, South Carolina, and took it.
Lafayette helped muster French forces to offset such British victories.

intend to let the British furnish the transportation. In his year with the U.S. forces he had learned how to be slippery, and he easily avoided the British traps.

Congress granted Lafayette a furlough, and he sailed for France in January, 1779. In Paris and at the king's palace at Versailles he was the hero of the hour. He was embraced by all the king's ministers and kissed by all the queen's ladies. And Adrienne and his daughter hugged him hardest of all. For a year he consulted, advised, and made a thousand plans to crush the British. But the center of action was not the French court but the American battlefields. He returned to the United Sates in the spring of 1780.

Lafayette brought with him the warmly welcomed promise of more French aid. The help was sorely needed, for the war was going badly for Washington. The English had scored notable victories at Savannah, Georgia, and Charleston, South Carolina, and were threatening Northern positions held by the Americans. Lafayette served as Washington's chief aide in dealing with the French forces and their commanders.

But for long months the French remained in Newport, Rhode Island, reluctant to move against the British unless they were backed up by their own fleet. The French fleet, however, preferred to linger in the French West Indies. Washington restored Lafayette to his old command of the Virginia Division and sent him south to harry the troops of Lord Cornwallis.

Cornwallis was contemptuous of this "boy" commander. Yet the "boy" was able to trick Cornwallis into extending his lines until they ran into a solid line of Pennsylvania regiments commanded by General Anthony Wayne. Then it was Cornwallis's turn to retreat. The British withdrew from Richmond, Virginia, and barricaded themselves at Yorktown, on Chesapeake Bay.

Lafayette's Virginia Division pinned down Cornwallis until massive aid came. And it did—the French fleet from the Indies, the French army from Rhode Island, and Washington's main force gathered from a dozen staging areas. They laid siege to Cornwallis's position—and the British surrendered. "The play is over," wrote Lafayette in a letter home. "The fifth act is just ended."

The war was over, but not Lafayette's great love for America. He helped the struggling United States to obtain foreign loans and its farmers and merchants to find foreign outlets for their goods. In 1784 he spent six months in America, visiting old comrades and enjoying the acclaim of the public.

But Lafayette fell afoul of the French Revolution that began in 1789. He was in jail for five years and stripped of his fortune. To help him, the United States Congress voted him the pay he had refused to accept while in service. Now the money was welcome. Congress also granted him a tract of 11,520 acres in Louisiana, but it was a long time before the land furnished any income.

In 1824 President James Monroe invited Lafayette to visit the United States once more. For more than a year he was cheered, toasted, and made much of by the American people. They poured out their affection and esteem everywhere that Lafayette traveled in the now-peaceful land.

Lafayette lived for another decade. He engaged in politics, made speeches, and fought for liberal causes. When he died in 1834, his grave was sodded with earth from Bunker Hill, site of one of the first great battles of the American Revolution.

In the hall of America's heroes, old Ben Franklin stands in the first rank. NEW YORK PUBLIC LIBRARY

1778—"...to maintain effectually the liberty, sovereignty and independence absolute and unlimited, of the said United States..."

Ben Franklin was seventy, old and tired. Gout had lamed him badly. Yet here in the autumn of 1776 he was aboard the *Reprisal,* sailing for France. His body protested the strain, but his mind and heart were ready for the task. As he had been doing for decades, he was again serving his country.

This mission was perhaps the most important in Franklin's long public career. His assignment was to bring France into the American Revolution, fighting on the side of the brand-new United States. France's help, as it turned out, was vital. Only with the aid of French troops and ships was Washington finally able to bottle up the British at Yorktown and effect a cease-fire and an end to the war.

But that victory took place in 1781, five long years after the time when Franklin started on his way to France to ask for help. Old Ben Franklin was no stranger to Europe—he had served as a colonial agent on and off in England for eighteen years.

At home he had seen the Revolution begin, had observed how desperately American leaders worked for the Declaration of Independence and for a sense of unity among the thirteen former colonies. Franklin knew at once that America could never win the war alone. Victory would come only when the infant nation was backed from abroad with military supplies and with a strong navy. Without these, America's army could never conquer the British.

Even before the Declaration was published on July 4, 1776, before the colonies proclaimed themselves a nation, Franklin was head of the Committee of Secret Correspondence, set up by the Continental Congress. Its task was to make friends with foreign nations and arrange for their help. Franklin was an old hand at this work. His patience and cunning were immense. And he could charm anyone who came into his orbit.

Long before, as a colonial agent in London during the 1760's, he had quietly arranged for Dutch, French, and even British arms makers to smuggle guns to the colonies. He had kept up his arrangements until he returned to America in 1775. Thanks to his undercover work, the colonial troops had enough arms and gunpowder to hold their own when the fighting started on that historic 18th of April in '75.

Now, in the late autumn of 1776, the *Reprisal* anchored in Quiberon Bay, France. Franklin, ashore, took a post chaise to the city of Nantes at the mouth of the Loire River. He was delighted to find goods of all kinds piled high on the Nantes docks ready for shipment to America. It was the same story at other French ports—they were shipping to the United States all sorts of vitally needed stores. The link between the peoples of the two nations was strong.

But as Franklin already well knew, the link between the governments of the two countries was considerably weaker. Then, as now, governments were deeply involved in the game of "power politics." France was interested in helping the United States mainly as a way to weaken its old rival and enemy, Britain. France was not ready to back a loser—as the United States might very well turn out to be.

It was Franklin's task to convince the French king, Louis XVI, and his ministers that with French help, the American Revolution would succeed. That success, Franklin was ready to demonstrate, would enable France to triumph over Britain without an open declaration of war. With his American associate commissioners, Silas Deane and Arthur Lee, Franklin set about to win the French government over to the side of the United States.

All this had to be done while France was maintaining relations with Britain. There were British diplomats—and British spies—all over France, reporting on every move the three American commissioners made. The work was further complicated by the fact that through late 1776 and virtually all of 1777, U.S. forces won very few battles. It looked as though France was being asked to back a lost cause.

But such was the force of Franklin's arguments—and such was the attraction of his great personality—that he managed to keep the talks going for a year or more without letting the French government back away. French men admired him for his achievements in science—and French women loved him for his charm and sweetness. In France, Franklin was an eighteenth century version of "Mr. America," even though he was in his seventies.

Then on December 1, 1777, wonderful news arrived in France. The forces of American General Horatio Gates had scored a stunning upset victory over British troops under General "Gentleman Johnny" Burgoyne at the Battle of Saratoga in upstate New York. It was just what was needed to bring France into open cooperation with the United States.

The Treaty of Alliance with France was signed February 6, 1778. Its Article II stated: "The essential and direct end of the present defensive alliance is to maintain effectually the liberty, sovereignty and independence absolute and un-limited, of the said United States, as well in matters of govern-ment as of commerce." With the signing, France went on to support the U.S. forces with troops and naval vessels leading to the surrender at Yorktown. Franklin was a hero to the French for bringing them this opportunity to help the Amer-icans—and to strike a blow against the British.

For that matter, Franklin had long been a hero to his fellow countrymen. Born in Boston in 1706, he was the fifteenth child and youngest son in a brood of seventeen children. His father made soap and candles, and ten-year-old Ben, after a couple of years of school, began work in his father's shop. Soon the boy was apprenticed to his older brother James, a printer. Ben became a good printer, too— and taught himself to be a good writer as well. In addition, the boy studied on his own most of the natural and physical sciences, mathematics, navigation, grammar, logic, and several languages.

The American victory at the Battle of Saratoga brought French aid to the new nation. Franklin had patiently laid the groundwork for this French-U.S. accord. NEW YORK PUBLIC LIBRARY

*Franklin proved that lightning was electricity by a simple experiment.
He flew a kite in a thunderstorm, and attracted lightning (electricity)
down the wet kite string to a metal key at the end of the string.*

But Ben got himself in trouble with his brother. Writing several newspaper articles, he signed them with the fictitious name of "Mrs. Silence Dogood" and put them under the door into the printshop. James liked the pieces and printed them— until he found out that Ben was the author. Then he and Ben quarreled, and the apprentice soon quit.

Quitting Boston as well, Ben struck out for Philadelphia. He soon found work as a printer and gradually rose in his profession. At twenty-four he owned his own shop and acted as printer and publisher for his own paper, *The Pennsylvania Gazette*. He even wrote much of the paper himself. That same year he married Deborah Read, and in time they had four children.

BENJAMIN FRANKLIN

The Pennsylvania Gazette, which he continued to publish for thirty-seven years, was one of the most widely read papers in the colonies. Yet far more successful was his *Poor Richard's Almanac,* published from 1733 to 1758. It contained such popular homilies as "Early to bed, early to rise, makes a man healthy, wealthy, and wise." Franklin was always in good health, became modestly rich, and was accounted one of the sharpest men in America. But he went to bed late and got up when he pleased. He rarely took his own advice.

His printing business prospering, Franklin soon found he had time for public service. He became postmaster of Philadelphia in 1737, and fifteen years later, deputy postmaster general for all the colonies. He set up practices and systems of sorting and delivering mail that have lasted to this day— although they worked better in his time. He installed a subscription library in Philadelphia, and established the city's first hospital and fire department.

Franklin was interested in the public good, but he had

time left over for other favorite pursuits—science and invention. He proved that lightning is electricity, then installed the first lightning rods on his own house. He invented the fuel-saving "Franklin stove" to replace the wasteful open fireplace. He also invented bifocal eyeglasses. He charted the flow of the Gulf Stream in the Atlantic Ocean. The scientific world honored him for his discoveries.

Franklin's major contributions to his country, however, were to be political. These began in 1754 when he offered his Albany Plan of Union to the colonies. This plan was a call to unite for defense against the French and hostile Indians and for some self-government among the colonies. Although some features of the Albany Plan later became part of the U.S. Constitution, the plan itself did not win adoption at the time.

Three years later the Pennsylvania colonial legislature asked Franklin to represent the colony in London on a tax problem. He stayed in Britain, with some short trips home, for the next eighteen years. A highlight of his stay occurred in 1766 when he appeared before Parliament to answer a total of 174 questions dealing with the colonial protest against the Stamp Act. His clear and logical answers helped convince the British that they were wrong in trying to impose the Act on the colonies.

Back in America two weeks after Lexington and Concord, Franklin was one of the men who worked with Jefferson on the Declaration of Independence. In the fall of 1776, he was off to France to perform his greatest service to his country.

Remaining in France to sign the final peace treaty with Britain in 1783, Franklin came home to stay in 1785. But his service to his country was not over. He acted as president of the Pennsylvania executive council, a post something like that of governor, for two years. In the summer of 1787 he was a delegate to the Constitutional Convention that met in Philadelphia. Old age and disability prevented him from speaking from the floor. But his speeches, read by others, were wise and powerful arguments for the U.S. Constitution that was finally adopted.

Franklin died in 1790 at the age of eighty-four. To the last he was a simple man, despite his successes and the honors bestowed upon him. Typical of his simplicity was the fact that, unlike most of the important men around him, he never wore a wig. And he began his last will and testament with the words: "I, Benjamin Franklin, printer . . ."

BENJAMIN FRANKLIN

Cheerful Baron von Steuben brought discipline and method to the willing but wild American troops. NEW YORK PUBLIC LIBRARY

1778—"...an old blanket or woolen bedcover..."

Geneal George Washington was a magnificent leader of men, a brilliant military strategist, a shrewd politician able to wangle arms and supplies from a reluctant Congress. Yet his own army training and experience had been catch-as-catch-can. Not until an old professional soldier took over was the Continental Army thoroughly trained in elementary military skills.

That old professional soldier was a German named Friedrich Wilhelm Ludolf Gerhard Augustin, Baron von Steuben. The "von" had been tacked on to the family name by his grandfather eager for high social rank—and the "Baron" had been added by Steuben himself, also because he wanted to enhance his social prestige.

Steuben first presented himself to Ben Franklin and Silas Deane, the American commissioners in Paris, and they enlarged on the description. They gave him letters of introduction to General Washington in which Steuben was described as a lieutenant general only recently retired from service under Frederick the Great of Prussia. Actually Steuben had ranked no higher than captain—and he had been forcibly retired from the Prussian army fourteen years before.

But for all that, Steuben was an honest man. When he landed in America—at Portsmouth, N. H., on December 1, 1777—he immediately wrote Washington that he wanted to serve under him. What was more, he was willing to serve as a volunteer with no rank and, for the present, no salary other than expenses. If the Americans did not win the Revolution or if the Baron's performance did not prove satisfactory, he wanted nothing more. If the Americans did win and Steuben measured up to his own claims, then he would expect suitable compensation.

Washington, delighted with the offer, invited Steuben to join him at Valley Forge, Pennsylvania, where the main body of American forces had holed up for the winter. Steuben arrived at Valley Forge on a blustery February day in 1778. He was appalled and dismayed by what he found.

There were about 9,000 men in the camp, and 4,000 of them were without even substitutes for proper clothing and shoes. The officers themselves appeared at parade formations in, as Steuben later wrote, "a sort of dressing-gown, made of an old blanket or woolen bed-cover." Without adequate clothing, the soldiers huddled around roaring fires all day to keep warm. A pro-British newspaper published in New York City taunted Congress by saying that it would always have rags for making paper money—the army would be able to supply enough.

"The arms at Valley Forge were in a horrible condition, covered with rust, half of them without bayonets, many from which a single shot could not be fired," Steuben recorded. The horses had no grain or hay and could not graze on the snow-covered pastures. As a result, the animals died in great numbers, and the army could not haul in its own supplies. The few wagon teams that Congress eventually got around to furnishing did little to relieve the shocking shortages.

Washington's forces lacked clothing and shoes, food for the men and fodder for the horses, equipment, arms, and ammunition. Worse, the army lacked organization, discipline, training. What was not lacking, surprisingly enough, was spirit.

Appointed acting Inspector General, Steuben set about to build a disciplined army which still retained its spirit. Time was critically short, Steuben realized, for when spring came the army had to be ready to move against the enemy. "In our European armies a man who has been drilled for three months is called a recruit. Here, in two months I must have a soldier," he said.

He said it, of course, in German. Steuben knew no English when he came to America at the age of forty-eight, and he never learned more than he needed to make his meaning understood. To the end, his "English" was mixed with a wild melange of French and German, and spiced with plenty of profanity from all three languages. But the American army liked this fat, balding, cheerful leader, and the men proceeded to learn what he had to teach.

Under Frederick the Great, Steuben had absorbed the discipline of fear. He sensed at once that the American troops could not be coerced or cowed into obedience. He had to prove to them logically why obedience and discipline were necessary.

In a letter to an old army friend in Europe, he said, "You say to your soldier, 'Do this' and he does it. But I must say, 'This is the reason why you ought to do that,' and then he does it." Thus Steuben relied less on what Frederick the Great had taught and more on his own experience in leading a corps of volunteers in the Seven Years War.

Steuben took over the training of the Valley Forge army about the middle of March, 1778. His first pupils formed a special company selected from the whole force. He taught them how to march in step, how to dress right and left to form an even line. Within two weeks Steuben was ready to report that his selected company "knew perfectly how to bear arms, had a military air, knew how to march, to form in column, deploy, and execute . . . maneuvers with excellent precision." Gradually his instructions extended through the entire Valley Forge force.

The baron took one cue from his old mentor, Frederick the Great. The Prussian warrior-king had preached that the best offensive infantry weapon was the bayonet. The American soldier had always been a good marksman, but his only use for a bayonet was as a spit for broiling a beefsteak over an open fire. Steuben ordered drill and more drill with the bayonet until the troops were competent and confident in its use.

Steuben's teachings extended beyond the drill field into every corner of army life. He taught the men how to assume their posts at guard duty (and made them stay awake on guard) and instructed the officers on punctuality. He made

That Valley Forge winter was the time for Steuben to teach American soldiers how to fire, retreat, and reload—all on command.

With the rank of major general, Steuben rides proudly in his post as Inspector General of all U.S. forces.

the "noncoms" set a standard of personal neatness, and he counseled the lowest privates to keep themselves and their campsite clean.

On May 6, 1778, Washington's forces celebrated the news of the alliance with France. At the same time Washington announced Steuben's Congressional appointment as Inspector General of the entire U.S. Army, with the pay and rank of a major general. The next month Washington's forces put Steuben's teachings to the test in the Battle of Monmouth, in New Jersey. Neither the British nor the Americans really won that engagement, but the Americans fought with superb discipline and superior tactics against much stronger forces. Steuben passed his test at Monmouth.

Partly because Steuben was a foreigner, Washington did not want to let him lead troops in battle. Others—notably Lafayette of France and Kosciusko of Poland—were distinguishing themselves as fighting leaders. But for some reason, Washington did not care to give Steuben the responsibility of command in battle. Washington, however, recommended that Steuben be given complete charge of training all American forces.

To carry out this assignment Steuben wrote (and had translated from German to English) a book called *Regulations for the Order and Discipline of the Troops of the United States*. It was partly based on the old Prussian system, altered to meet the changing conditions of the American Revolution. Steuben did retain the emphasis on the offensive use of the bayonet. This proved especially useful when the Americans under General Anthony Wayne attacked the British at Stony Point, New York, on July 16, 1779, and again in the final assault on Yorktown, Virginia, on October 14, 1781.

Although Steuben was not given battle command, he helped General Robert Howe defend West Point, New York, in June, 1780. In October of that same year he assisted General Nathaniel Greene in Virginia and the Carolinas, and when the peace was signed in 1783, he helped demobilize the American forces.

By this time Steuben had been soldiering for most of his life, and he was tired. Born at Madgeburg, Prussia, in 1730, he had entered the army at sixteen. At nineteen he was already a commissioned officer and in 1756, at the outbreak of the Seven Years War, he was a first lieutenant in a crack regiment. He was wounded at least three times in that war and once, for several months, was a prisoner of the Russians.

BARON VON STEUBEN

At war's end, he was mustered out of the army—perhaps because he had no title of nobility. (This was when he added "Baron" to his name.) Until the American Revolution, he served in the courts of several petty German states. Then came his last chance for military glory—and he took it.

After the Revolution, Steuben had to wage another war —this one with Congress for a settlement of claims to money he considered was owing him. This "war" took years, and Steuben was never wholly satisfied with the final settlement. He eventually retired to an estate in New York's Mohawk Valley. He died there in 1794, fully deserving his enduring title of "Drillmaster of the Revolution."

Benedict Arnold. Largely a victim of his own ambition, Arnold betrayed his country's trust in him. NEW YORK PUBLIC LIBRARY

1780—"Arnold has betrayed us! Whom can we trust now?"

"Sir:

"Inclosed you'll receive a parcel of papers taken from a certain John Anderson who has a pass signed by General Arnold as may be seen. The Papers were found under the feet of his stockings. . . ."

The letter (dated September 23, 1780, at Tarrytown, New York) was addressed to General Washington and signed by Lieutenant Colonel John Jameson of the Second Light Dragoons of the Continental Army. The "General Arnold" mentioned in the note was Benedict Arnold, Washington's trusted (until then) commander of the fortress at West Point, New York, on the bluffs of the Hudson River. "John Anderson" was in reality Major John André, a British spy.

The "parcel of papers" was made up of documents in

Benedict Arnold's handwriting, documents that recorded secret war material known only to the highest U.S. officers, plus pages of notes on West Point that would be highly important to the British. The notes included information on the fort's 3,000 defenders.

The "parcel of papers" was clear-cut proof that General Benedict Arnold had committed treason. Washington was thunderstruck. All he could say was, "Arnold has betrayed us! Whom can we trust now?"

Washington was saddened and dismayed by this proof of treachery. Arnold, one of his ablest generals, had sold out to the British—and indeed had already escaped to British-held New York City. There was nothing else to do but to proceed with the trial against Major André on spy charges.

André was tried before a board of general officers, to whom the British officer made a complete and candid confession of guilt. He was sentenced to death by hanging. Despite the real sympathy that this likeable young officer evoked from his American captors, the sentence was carried out.

And what of Arnold? Why did he deceive Washington? Why did he betray his country and his cause? The reasons for his treachery are hidden in the maze of his complex character and personality.

Born in Norwich, Connecticut, in 1740, Benedict Arnold was the son of the town drunk. As a teenager Arnold served in the French and Indian War, deserting twice when the pace of the war proved too slow. The war over, he served as a young captain on merchant ships long enough to accumulate money to go into business. The first such business was a combined bookstore and apothecary's shop (drugstore) in New Haven, Connecticut. Later he traded widely in all sorts of merchandise, doing business in Canada and the West Indies as well as the colonies. He married and became the father of three sons.

At the outbreak of the Revolution, Arnold was commander of a local militia company. Once he heard the news of the fighting at Lexington and Concord, he could not be held back. With his men he forced open the town arsenal, grabbed powder and shot, and was off to Boston.

Arnold quickly won a colonel's commission and an assignment to storm the British-held Fort Ticonderoga in western Massachusetts (on the present-day New York-Vermont border). The prize was to be the fort's cannon, desperately needed by the colonies. But Colonel Ethan Allen was already assembling his Green Mountain Boys for their own assault on Ticonderoga.

This bothered Arnold not the slightest. He first demanded that command of the Green Mountain Boys be turned over to him, although he finally settled for a shared command with Allen. The two led a successful raid on Ticonderoga and marched into the fort together. But Arnold and Allen soon quarreled, and Arnold was forced to go back to Boston alone.

Arnold had many problems. His wife had just died, leaving his three young sons without a mother. He had put up some of his own money to finance the Ticonderoga campaign, and the Massachusetts Committee of Public Safety, the governing authority, was reluctant to pay him back. But Arnold had a grand plan in mind, one calculated to win him top honors in the eyes of Washington and the Continental Congress.

The scheme was this: Arnold would lead an expedition to

It was the capture of British spy John André that revealed Arnold's treachery. LIBRARY OF CONGRESS

"In the name of the Great Jehovah and the Continental Congress,"
Colonel Ethan Allen (Arnold's co-commander) announces his presence
to the British commandant of Fort Ticonderoga. NEW YORK PUBLIC LIBRARY

attack Quebec, Britain's Canadian stronghold. Its success would enlist the French-Canadians on the colonial side. The idea was not new, but Arnold's planned route to Quebec was. He would not lead his force by way of Lake George and Lake Champlain. Instead, he would enter the Kennebec River at its Atlantic mouth. Then he would sail upriver through the desolate Maine woods, over to the Dead River, and finally to Quebec.

Congress authorized the expedition, and Washington appointed Arnold as its leader. Arnold ordered two hundred small riverboats to be built, and he and his thousand men reached the mouth of the Kennebec River on September 22, 1775. Arnold estimated it would take twenty days to reach Quebec.

But everything went wrong. The new boats leaked badly. The uncharted river proved to be studded with falls and rapids which had to be portaged. The food ran out, and the men were reduced to eating candles and shoe leather. The expedition, now down to seven hundred men, finally reached the St. Lawrence River opposite Quebec, on November 9. It had taken forty-five days instead of the estimated twenty.

Nevertheless the men were in good spirits. Arnold's forces were enlarged by three hundred troops under General Montgomery, fresh from their capture of Montreal. They brought food, clothing, and arms. A combined assault led by Arnold and Montgomery in late December on the walled city of Quebec failed, however. Montgomery was killed and more than half the Americans were captured or slain.

Arnold withdrew and made winter camp a little distance from the city. He begged Congress for reinforcements, which did not arrive until April, 1776. By that time the British,

*Arnold lowers himself, hand over hand, from his burning schooner
at Valcour Island.* NEW YORK PUBLIC LIBRARY

At Saratoga Arnold distinguished himself by valiant charges against British forces. NEW YORK PUBLIC LIBRARY

also reinforced, drove the Americans south in a rout. Arnold's Canadian effort was a complete failure.

Next Arnold led a makeshift fleet of lake schooners against the British on Lake Champlain. The British were threatening to take Crown Point, New York, and Arnold's plan was to block the British vessels at Valcour Island. Arnold's schooners were sunk—although they succeeded in preventing the enemy from seizing Crown Point.

Arnold, by now a major general in spite of his defeats, bounced back in 1777. Two British armies, under General "Gentleman Johnny" Burgoyne and Colonel Barry St. Leger, were marching on Albany, New York (a third force under Lord Howe was supposed to move north from New York to join them, but never got started). At Fort Stanwick, near present-day Rome, New York, Arnold tricked St. Leger's Indian allies into thinking he had a superior force, and the Indians fled.

Then at Saratoga Arnold led a pick-up group into murderous attacks on Burgoyne's seasoned troops. It was the colonial victory at Saratoga that persuaded the French to come into the war on the American side. It was also a personal victory for Arnold, who won high praise from Congress.

The British had retreated from Philadelphia, and after Saratoga, Washington named Arnold as commandant of the city. There the thirty-nine-year-old Arnold, a widower for several years, met Margaret "Peggy" Shippen, only nineteen and a society belle. They were married on April 8, 1779. Before their honeymoon was done, say some historians, Arnold had begun his task of treachery.

During the British occupation of Philadelphia, Peggy Shippen had been friendly with key army officers. When she

In this rather melodramatic picture, Arnold hands over the plans of the West Point fortifications. NEW YORK PUBLIC LIBRARY

expose "an honest man to the envy and jealousy of mankind at the same time that it lays him open to the malicious attacks of every dirty scoundrel that deals in the murder of reputations."

But, being honest, he also realized that he owed his prosperity to the government which was now asking for his help. So he took the job. At first he raised money largely on his own credit standing, rather than on any government promise to pay. He begged and borrowed enough to finance the Yorktown campaign, the battle which won the war for the United States. With the emergency funds, he bought arms, meat, flour, and rum, all in short supply.

At one point in the campaign the soldiers, who had been without pay for months, refused to march. Morris quickly borrowed $20,000 from a French financier and another $20,000 from business friends of his in Philadelphia. One soldier noted in his diary: "This day will be famous in the annals of history for being the first on which the troops of the United States received one month's pay in specie [gold]."

When he took office, Morris found the business affairs of the government in a chaotic state. Records, bills, invoices, and receipts were either missing or jumbled together in disorderly piles. But this was not the worst of the trouble. It did not take neat books to show that there was no money coming in. Proper business methods were needed, of course, but these by themselves could produce no funds. Thus Morris had two tasks: to *save* money by methodical business practices, and to *raise* money by showing that the U.S. government was a good credit risk.

Saving money was the easier task of the two. Morris bought supplies for the entire army, thus cutting out the extravagant

[163]

In colonial times there were no standard coins, and foreign coins from nearly every country in the Old World were in circulation. This is a French coin (shown front and back) used in the colonies before the War, in 1767.

Various states attempted to mint their own coins to alleviate the confusion. This is a cent minted by the State of New Jersey in 1787.

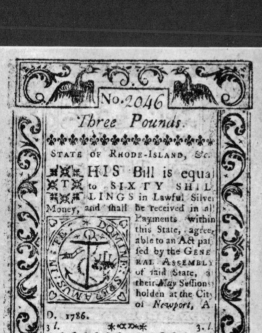

In order to finance the Revolution, the Continental Congress had to issue paper money—it had no power to levy taxes. By 1780 the value of the Continental Note had fallen to 2½ cents per dollar. Finally, the Continental Congress stopped issuing the paper money, but the phrase, "not worth a Continental" —meaning something has no value— is still used today. Here, a Continental Note, 1786.

As late as 1813, the English guinea was still in circulation in the U.S.

The new Constitution gave the Federal Government the exclusive right to mint coins, although it made no provision for the control or issue of paper money. This is a ten-dollar gold piece of 1795.

A 25¢-piece of 1840.

and wasteful method of having each regiment buy its own. He himself hired and outfitted the merchant ships and privateers in government service. He cut down foolish spending by the military hospitals, and he installed a businesslike system of keeping books and records.

But raising money was difficult—almost impossible. Other than foreign loans, the one big source of funds was the tax revenues. Only the states, however, could tax their people. It was up to each state to requisition taxes from its citizens, then voluntarily turn over the collections to the national government. At first Morris thought that if the people could only be made aware of the need, they would pay their state taxes and press their state governments to forward them to the national treasury. He tried to tell the people—but got no response.

Then he wrote letters to the state legislatures. These produced no results, either. He sent his own men to the legislatures in session. The legislatures refused to hear their pleas. Washington joked that the states believed "that the Army had contracted such a habit of encountering distress and difficulties, and of living without money, that it would be impolitic and injurious to introduce other customs in it!"

After the Yorktown victory the fighting was over, but the peace treaty was not yet written. Until it was, the army could not be disbanded. Morris had to turn again to France and Holland for funds, especially to the former. France had been generous so far. Up to 1780 it had furnished about 9,000,000 *livres*. In 1781 alone France advanced 14,000,000 *livres* to the United States.

Although the French government was dissatisfied with the money situation in the United States, it continued to help out. For his part, Morris took two bold steps towards curing the trouble. First he persuaded Congress to abandon the almost worthless paper money and to use only specie as currency. Then he organized the Bank of North America. Although under private control, the Bank of North America handled all financial matters for the U.S. government. The bank was backed by a $400,000 load from France.

Morris did not think that the Revolutionary War generation should have to pay all the bills while leaving future generations to enjoy all the advantages of victory and freedom. He was all for making the future bear the greater part of the expense, and he was convinced that a national debt was actually good for the country. He said, "A public debt, supported by public revenue, will prove the strongest cement to keep our [nation] together."

In many of his dealings with France and Holland, Morris was immeasurably aided by Haym Salomon. A Polish Jew, Salomon had fled Poland because he was persecuted as a freedom fighter in his native land. Love of freedom led him to the American struggle for independence. In Philadelphia he found he could best serve the cause by acting as banker and paymaster. It was Salomon who actually handled most of the French and Dutch loans as well as the pay for the French forces in America. He lent much of his own money to the U.S. government and to members of the armed forces. Morris considered his help invaluable.

Morris's own help to the U.S. government was equally invaluable, even though his own company continued to profit from the war. Born in Liverpool, England, in 1734, he came to Maryland at the age of thirteen. His father, already in the colony, was a tobacco exporter. The boy soon went to

[167]

work for the Willing Company, an import-export firm in Philadelphia. By the time he was twenty he was a partner.

Caught up in the protest against the Stamp Act in 1765, Morris served on the committee that forced the Philadelphia stamp tax collector to quit. It was the first time he got involved in public life. A decade later, after service in the Committee of Correspondence and the Pennsylvania Assembly, he was a member of the Continental Congress.

Morris was an active Congressman and at the same time a busy supplier of war needs. His fellow Congressmen honored him for both pursuits. For example, John Adams wrote General Horatio Gates:

You ask me what you are to think of Robt. Morris? . . . I think he has a masterly understanding, an open temper, and an honest heart. . . . He has vast designs in the mercantile way. And no doubt pursues mercantile ends, which are always gain; but he is an excellent member of our body.

Morris served as Superintendent of Finance from 1781 until 1784, a year after the peace treaty with Britain was signed. He was a delegate to the Constitutional Convention in 1787, the group that wrote the present charter of the United States. President Washington asked him to serve at the first Secretary of the Treasury. He declined, but accepted Pennsylvania's appointment as one of its first two U.S. Senators. He served in the U.S. Senate from 1789 to 1795.

But before his Senatorial term ended, Morris had tied up his very considerable fortune in land speculation and had borrowed much more as well. Then disaster struck. Napoleon Bonaparte launched his campaign to conquer Europe, money was tight, and bankers called in their loans. Morris had bought vast stretches of land in western New York and even a large tract of what is now Washington, D.C. He had counted on selling the land when prices went up. Instead, prices went down. Morris lost everything, and was deeply in debt.

Morris spent three and a half years in debtors' prison in Philadelphia. He was released only when he declared himself bankrupt—unable to pay. Sick and dispirited, he lived only until 1806. It was a sad ending for a man who had found money to keep his country going in its darkest days.

Drummers and a fifer playing "Yankee Doodle" lead American forces on a victory march. LIBRARY OF CONGRESS

1775-1783—The Common Soldier

There were brave captains and gallant commanders in the American Revolution, bold and daring leaders of men. But what of the men themselves, the ones who were being led? What kind of people were they? What kept them loyal to a cause that, for a long time, had little chance of winning out? What sort of man fought in the Revolution?

His parents may have come from Britain a year or a hundred and fifty years before, or their point of origin may have been France, Germany or Holland. He himself may have been a newcomer. He may have been Negro, mulatto, or Indian. Before he joined the army he may have been a farmer, fisherman, or frontiersman, a lawyer, laborer, or landowner. He may have been Catholic, Protestant, Jew, or of no faith at all. He may have been in his teens or pushing sixty.

But his ancestry, his job, his religion, his age did not matter any more. He was an American, and he was a soldier fighting to be free.

How did he serve in the Revolution? He was either a member of a state militia outfit, or he was a regularly enlisted soldier in the Continental Army. As a state militiaman he had signed up for three, six, or nine months of service. As a soldier in the Continental Army he had enlisted for three years or for the duration of the war. And that duration stretched from the opening gunfire at Lexington and Concord in 1775 to the peace signed in Paris in 1783, eight long years in all.

What kind of a soldier did this American make? He did not take kindly to discipline and routine. His natural inclination was to fight as he had formerly hunted wild game for his table—to silently stalk his prey and to pick him off without revealing himself, a guerrilla warfare method still in use. It took such men as Steuben to pound some discipline and close-order drill into his makeup, for there is a time when guerrilla tactics must be abandoned for massed assaults.

There were plenty of desertions, when men slipped back to their farms and families. There were even defections to the British side. For the most part, however, the American soldier remained motivated. He was ready to fight for another month, another year, or however long it would take to win.

Even today an army recruit's pay is meager, and during the Revolution it was even more so. A private got six and two-thirds dollars a month; a corporal, drummer, or fifer was paid seven and a third dollars; a sergeant drew a salary of

This old Currier and Ives print is called "Heroes of '76, Marching to the Fight." It was published in 1876, a hundred years after the depicted scene. LIBRARY OF CONGRESS

This romanticized portrait of Continental soldiers does not square with the facts—few soldiers were so elegantly uniformed. LIBRARY OF CONGRESS

eight dollars a month. But uncontrolled inflation gripped the young United States during the war. Many prices were as high as they are today, although the soldier's pay remained fixed. Many paydays were skipped altogether.

Most soldiers received no government-issued uniforms. It wasn't until 1782, a year before the peace treaty was signed and a year after the last battle had been fought, that Congress decided that uniforms were to be blue and red, lined with white. Through the war the men fought in the same clothes they had on when they were mustered for duty. They wore these until the rags would no longer cling to their backs and legs. Then they scrounged and scrabbled until they found slightly more serviceable garments to wear.

The men were not very well fed, either. According to government regulation, each soldier in camp or permanent quarters was to claim a daily ration of a pound of fish or beef or three fourths of a pound of pork; a pound of bread or flour; a pint of milk; a quart of cider or spruce beer; plus vegetables, rice, molasses, and vinegar. He was also to get an issue of soap and candles. Fighting or marching, he was to be allowed a pound of bread and a pound of meat every day.

Rarely, however, did the Revolutionary soldier receive anywhere near his full ration of chow, and many days he was issued nothing at all. From Valley Forge Washington wrote Congress a bitter letter, complaining that his army would either starve or scatter to pick up what food they could find.

The soldier's health was about as good as the medical science of the day would permit. Most medicines were of the kind that old wives or witchdoctors would prescribe,

[175]

*The Valley Forge winter was particularly hard on the common soldier.
Fire, food, and shelter were hard to come by, and uniforms and arms
were scarce.* NEW YORK PUBLIC LIBRARY

their ingredients unknown and their curative powers based on casual observation or hearsay. The standard treatments for most ills were bloodletting, purges, or blistering. A wound in the leg or arm often required amputation, performed without antiseptics or anesthesia. Instead, the wounded man was given a stiff dose of rum or whiskey and a bullet to bite on, to keep from screaming in agony.

Indeed, rum or whiskey (in small quantities, to be sure) was considered vital to good health. But Washington had his problem drinkers among the troops. He had to issue an order that no soldier was to be sold more than half a pint of "spirit" a day.

Even though they grumbled continually among themselves, most soldiers were seldom bothered by poor pay, poor food, poor medical care. They carried with them a strong and heartening mental picture of mother, wife, daughter, or sweetheart. American women, for the most part, were as patriotic at their fighting men. There were, of course, many women who spied or worked for the British, as well as the thousands of Loyalist women who thought the Revolutionary cause a mistake.

Nevertheless, most colonial women could be counted on. Those who stayed at home cooked food for their own men—if the men were still in reach of the family cooking fire—or for any passing troops. They nursed the ill and the wounded, their own men or strangers. They spun and wove and sewed cloth into uniforms, and they stood in stony, defiant silence when British raiding parties pillaged their fields and barns and houses.

Some women even trooped after their men. They straggled along the rear of the columns of marching soldiers and caught up with them at nightfall. None was ever too exhausted to prepare a hot meal over an open fire and help pitch a tent or a lean-to for the night. As might be expected, there were women of bad reputation among those who followed the army on the march. But there were also women whose love for their men carried them along on strange, wild errands and missions of mercy.

During the American Revolution about one fifth of all Americans were blacks, slave or free. What part did American Negroes play in the war?

In 1775 there were about 2,250,000 people in the American colonies. Of these some half million—roughly twenty percent—were blacks. The 1790 census counted about 60,000 free Negroes out of a total of 700,000. If 60,000 were free in 1790, there must have been at least 30,000 or 40,000 free blacks in 1775. Crispus Attucks, one of the Americans slain in the Boston Massacre of 1770, was a free Negro.

When General Washington took command of the American forces in Boston in 1775, he issued an order that reflected the general American attitude towards blacks at the time. Washington instructed recruiting officers not to enlist "any deserter from the ministerial [that is, British] army, nor any stroller, negro, or vagabond, or person suspected of being an enemy to the liberty of America, nor any under eighteen years of age." Washington was grouping blacks with tramps and traitors, and he was saying in so many words that they were not to be trusted to fight for America's freedom.

The result was that thousands of black slaves crossed over to the British side, attracted by the promise of being set free. Many became fighting men under the British flag. Seeing this, Washington soon retracted his order, if not his attitude.

S U P P L E M E N T to the
NEW-YORK GAZETTEER   No. 44.

PEACE! LIBERTY! and INDEPENDENCE!

PHILADELPHIA March 24, 1783.

YESTERDAY arrived, after a paffage of 32 days from Cadiz, a French floop of war commanded by M. de Quefne, with the agreeable intelligence of PEACE. The particular Articles refpecting this happy and glorious Event are as follows. The principle articles of the preliminaries of the Peace of the 20th January, 1783.

FRANCE to retain *Tobago* and *Senegal.*

FRANCE to reftore to GREAT-BRITAIN *Grenada, St. Vincents, Dominico* and *St. Chriftophers.*

St. Euftatia, Demarara, Barbice and *Ifiquibo* to be reftored to the DUTCH.

GREAT-BRITAIN to reftore to FRANCE, *Goree, St. Lucia, St. Pierre,* and *Miquelon.*

The fifhery of France and England on the Coaft of Newfoundland, to remain on the fame footing on which they were by the treaty of 1763, except that part of the Coaft *Cape Bonavefta* at *Cape St. Johns,* fhall belong to the Englifh.

FRANCE to be re-eftablifhed in the *Eaft-Indies,* as well in *Bengal,* as on the Eaft and Weft Coaft of the Peninfula, as regulated by the treaty 1763. The articles of preceeding treaties, concerning the demolifhing of *Dunkirk* to be fuppreffed.

SPAIN to retain *Minorca* and *Weft-Florida.*

GREAT-BRITAIN cedes *Eaft-Florida* to SPAIN.

An agreement to be entered into between Spain and Great-Britain, about the cutting of wood in the Bay of Honduras.

GREAT-BRITAIN to retain the Dutch Settlements of *Negapatam* in the *Eaft-Indies.*

GREAT-BRITAIN to reftore *Trinquemale* to the DUTCH, if not retaken.

St. Euftatia, Demarara, and *Ifiquibo* to be reftored by the FRENCH to the UNITED PROVINCES.

GREAT-BRITAIN acknowledges the Sovereignty & Independence of the UNITED STATES of AMERICA.

The Limits of the UNITED STATES to be agreed upon in the provifional articles between them and Great-Britain, except that they fhall not extend further down the river Miffifippi than the 32d degree of North Latitude, from whence a line is to be drawn to the head of the River St. Mary, and along the middle of that river down to its mouth.

"Great Britain acknowledges the Sovereignty & Independence of the United States of America" was the key clause in this bulletin announcing the declaration of peace between the two countries.

"I was there, I was there!" says this proud old Revolutionary veteran to his young grandson. And patriotic pride has been an American quality for two centuries now. LIBRARY OF CONGRESS

In the end about 5,000 Negroes served in the American armed forces.

Many served with great distinction. In the early engagements, despite Washington's ban on Negro recruitment, blacks fought hard and well. Prince Estabrook was killed at Lexington, and Pomp Blackman skirmished there. Salem Poor saw action at Concord and Bunker Hill, and served at White Plains and Valley Forge. Peter Salem was in the front lines at Lexington, Concord, and Bunker Hill. Others fought valiantly in later battles.

But there was always a good deal of resentment against the blacks from both Northern and Southern states. One observer, writing about a Massachusetts regiment, noted: "Even in this regiment there were a number of negroes, which to persons unaccustomed to such associations, had a disagreeable, degrading effect." In time, however, blacks were accepted in the ranks of American Revolutionary troops, sometimes without open prejudice but more often grudgingly. There was still a long wait before they could win even the tokens and the crumbs of equality.

The way of the common soldier, white or black, has always been hard. Today's "GI Bill of Rights" does much to help the discharged soldier re-enter civilian life, but veterans of the American Revolution were offered no such help. True, Congress voted a discharge bonus of eighty dollars to each veteran. But Congress had no cash and could only pass out IOU certificates as payment. Many soldiers sold their certificates at once for a fraction of their value. Others, their enlistment records fouled up, were unable even to collect the certificates. They left for home, ragged and hungry and without a "farthing of money" in their pockets.

[181]

Each man, however, took home with him a sense of victory that was to sustain him in the difficult days ahead. He might have been unaware of the dimensions of freedom and independence that his new nation had achieved. But he had fought in a war, he had done his best, and he had triumphed. It was a story he could tell his children and they could tell their children down to the end of time.

Index

Revere, Paul, 63-71
Rights of Man, 116
Rush, Bejamin, 114
Russian Revolution, 119
Rutledge, Edward, 94

Salem, Peter, 181
Salomon, Haym, 167
Saratoga, Battle of, 134, 157
Sassamon, 11
Second Continental Congress, 50, 73-74
Secret Correspondence, Committee of, 132
Seven Years War, *See* French and Indian War
Sherman, Roger, 94
Sons of Liberty, 28, 42, 55, 63
Stamp Act, 27-28, 53, 58, 134
    See also Taxation
St. Leger, Barry, 157
Sugar Act, 20, 22, 25, 27-28
    See also Taxation

Taxation, 20, 22, 24-25, 53
    See also various tax acts
Tea Act, 54-55, 60
Townshend Act, 25, 53-54, 58
    See also Taxation
"triangular" trade, 20

United States Constitution, 39, 87

973.3
H

Hayman, LeRoy

Leaders of the
American Revolution